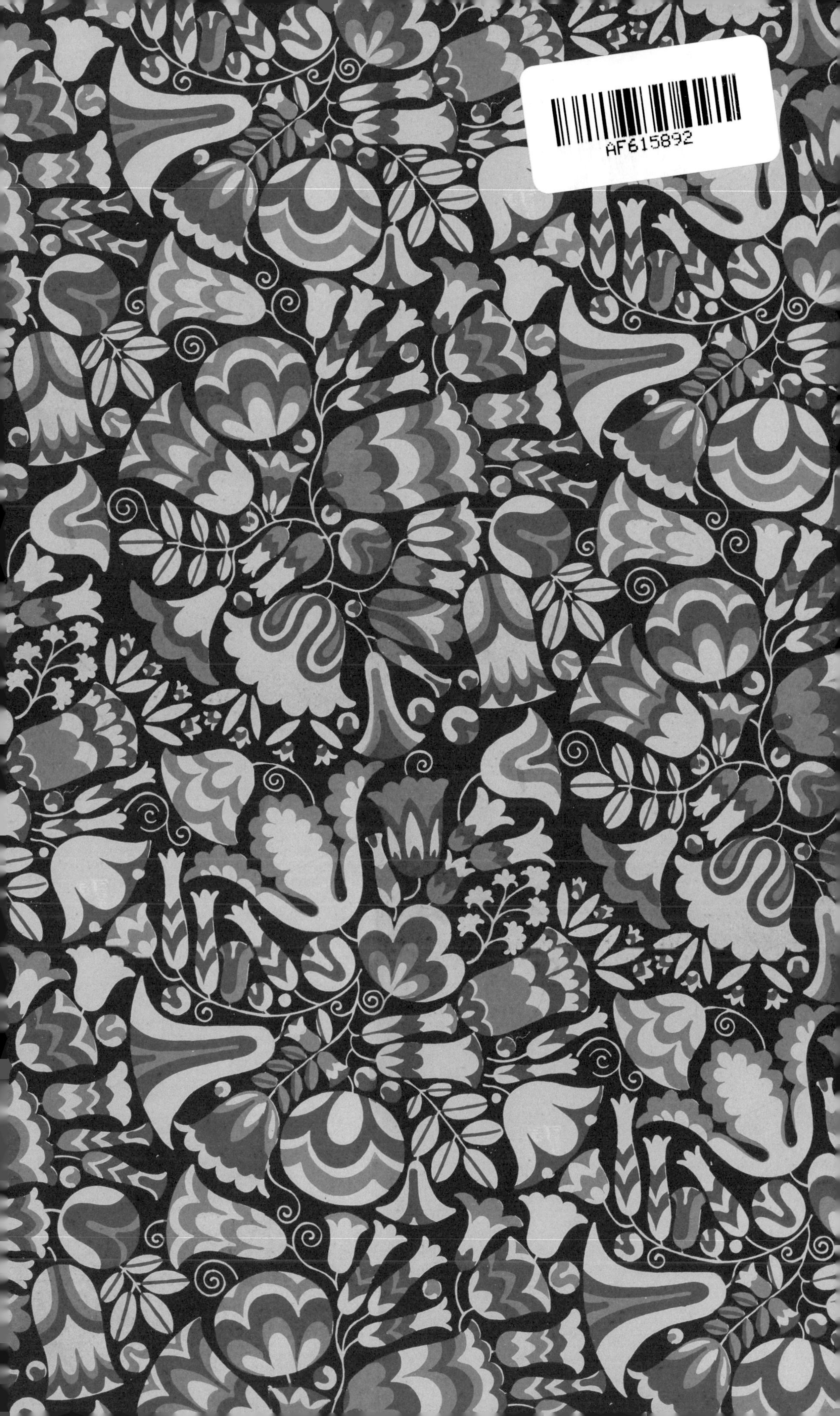

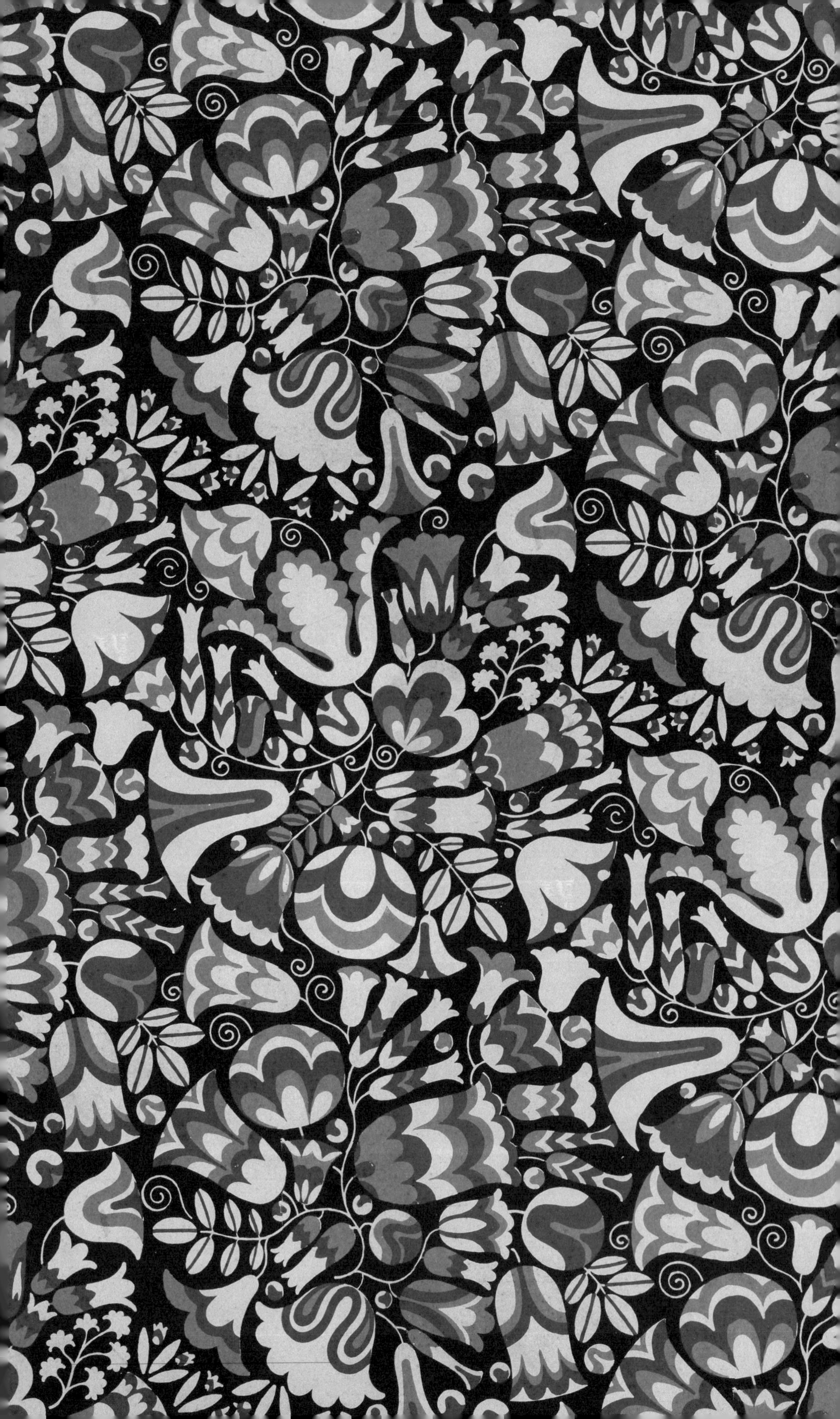

THE WITTGENSTEIN VITRINE

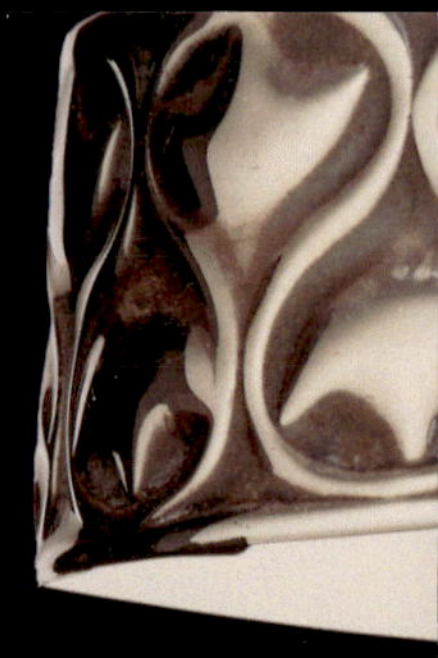

THE WITTGENSTEIN VITRINE

MODERN OPULENCE IN VIENNA

KEVIN W. TUCKER

WITH CONTRIBUTIONS BY FRAN BAAS AND
ELISABETH SCHMUTTERMEIER

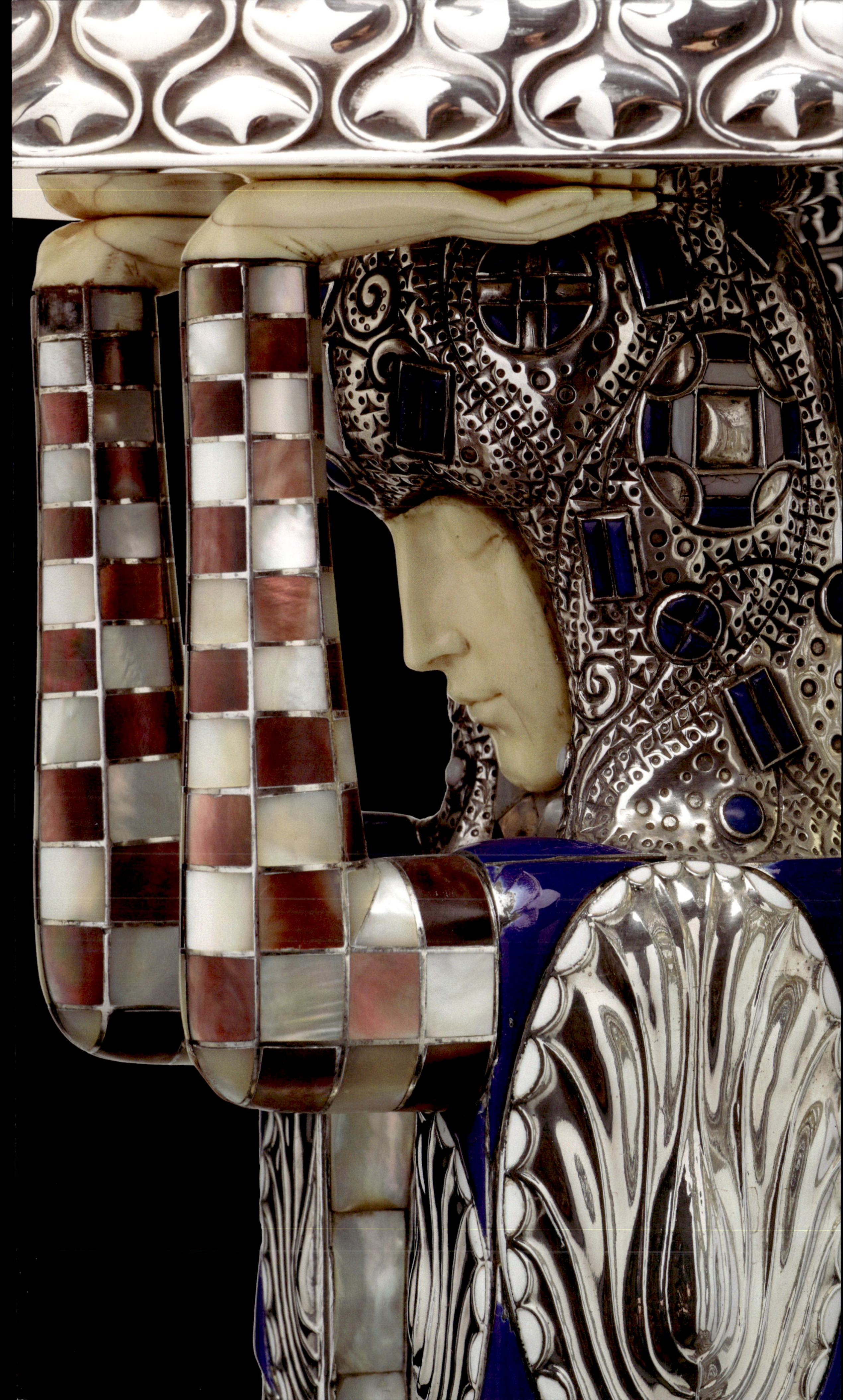

The silversmiths find themselves in the last stages of insanity as a result of working on your vitrine.

—Fritz Waerndorfer, letter to Carl Otto Czeschka, May 19, 1908

CONTENTS

DIRECTOR'S FOREWORD

The world will never understand what loving work went into making it.

—Fritz Waerndorfer, letter to Carl Otto Czeschka, May 19, 1908

Among the most compelling works of art are those that not only reflect the highest levels of aesthetic and technical achievement but also carry an artist's vision, embodying a larger identity of their cultural milieu within a moment in time—the *Zeitgeist*. Even more rarely, such a work arrives at a nexus where the efforts and perceptions of designer and maker, as well as public and critical interests, intersect in the realization and immediate recognition of such a masterpiece. The Wittgenstein Vitrine is one such work, lauded on its first appearance at Vienna's Kunstschau in 1908 and now revealed and celebrated anew as a defining object and the embodiment of a defining moment, in the collection of the Dallas Museum of Art and the three-decades-long history of its decorative arts and design program.

This publication serves as an acknowledgment of the importance of this monumental silver object and a recognition of our ongoing efforts to acquire, care for, and interpret great works of art. Over the past twenty-five years, the DMA has assembled an unparalleled collection of nineteenth- and twentieth-century American silver that has allowed the Museum to foster a greater understanding of craft, industry, and style through this particular lens. In keeping with our efforts to provide a broader international context for progressive design, the decorative arts and design program here has expanded over the past decade to include early modern objects from Europe and elsewhere in a variety of media. It is our belief that the Wittgenstein Vitrine, only rarely seen by the public since its creation, will now stand within this constellation of works as a guiding star and source of wonder and inspiration.

For his dedication in overseeing the acquisition, interpretation, and publication of the vitrine, we extend our sincere gratitude to Kevin W. Tucker, the Margot B. Perot Senior Curator of Decorative Arts and Design at the Dallas Museum of Art. In addition to his important scholarly efforts in researching the vitrine and organizing the symposium and exhibition, *Modern Opulence in Vienna: The Wittgenstein Vitrine,* he served as scholarly editor of both the print and online versions of the related catalogue and has written this volume's enlightening essay on the vitrine and its context within the Wiener Werkstätte and the oeuvre of the designer, Carl Otto Czeschka.

We offer our additional appreciation to Fran Baas, Associate Conservator at the DMA, for the conservation of the vitrine, detailed here in a revealing essay. Working with Mark Leonard, the Chief Conservator, and with Tucker, Baas undertook the technical analysis and meticulous eight-month treatment entailed in returning it to its original brilliance and grandeur. Our gratitude is also extended to Dr. Elisabeth Schmuttermeier, Curator, Metal Collection and Wiener Werkstätte Archive, MAK—Austrian Museum of Applied Arts/Contemporary Arts, Vienna—for her introduction to this publication and her stewardship of this important resource for scholars of early twentieth-century Viennese design.

For their contributions to the publication, we extend our gratitude to Frances Bowles, the catalogue editor; to Eric Zeidler, the DMA Publications Manager; to Brad Flowers, the DMA Head Photographer; to Ed Marquand, Melissa Duffes, Ryan Polich, who designed the catalogue, and the entire staff of Marquand Books; and to Patricia Fidler and Kate Zanzucchi, representing our distributors Yale University Press.

An expanded online version of the publication will be available on the DMA website in August 2016, with the additional essays previewing in December 2015. For the online publication, Dr. Alessandra Comini, University Distinguished Professor of Art History Emerita, Meadows School of the Arts, Southern Methodist University, contributed an essay on Vienna and the artistic and social context in which the vitrine was created. We are also fortunate to have an essay by Dr. Christian Witt-Dörring, Curator at MAK, on the Wiener Werkstätte. Dr. Samuel Albert, Adjunct Professor at the Fashion Institute of Technology, New York, contributed an essay devoted to Hungarian and other European design of the period. Dr. Christopher Long, Associate Professor at the University of Texas at Austin, School of Architecture, rounded out the online essays with a discussion of the legacy of the Wiener Werkstätte on modernism, specifically in the work of Josef Frank and Paul Frankl. We are pleased that Marquand Books will also be designing the online publication.

We are indebted to Ken and Debra Hamlett, David Owsley and the Alvin and Lucy Owsley Foundation, Cindy and Howard Rachofsky, and Nancy Shutt for making possible the presentation of *Modern Opulence: Art and Design in Early 20th-Century Vienna,* the DMA's symposium of

November 15, 2014, at which Tucker, Baas, and all the online contributors presented papers on various aspects of the Wittgenstein Vitrine.

The conservation and exhibition of the vitrine along with the accompanying publication were realized through the sustained efforts of Dallas Museum of Art staff members, each of whom proved indispensable to this ambitious undertaking: Jacqueline Allen, Jill Bernstein, Cynthia Calabrese, Giselle Castro-Brightenberg, Kimberlea Duran, Carol Griffin, Jessica Harden, Sara Hignite, Andrea Katz, John Lendvay, Stacey Lizotte, Ebony McFarland, Liz Menz, Olivier Meslay, Kelly Montana, Kevin Parmer, Alison Schwartzstein, Alison Silliman, Anne Smith, Isabel Stauffer, Rob Stein, Jenny Stone, Nicole Stutzman-Forbes, Joni Wilson-Bigornia, Tamara Wootton Forsyth, and Samantha Robinson. We extend special appreciation to our generous patrons and lenders for the *Modern Opulence* exhibition: Rita and Floyd Bucheit, Dr. Alessandra Comini, William Leazer and William Swann, Sidney and George Perutz, and those who choose to remain anonymous. To the Detroit Institute of Arts and our colleagues Dr. Graham Hood and Dr. Alan P. Darr and to the Saint Louis Art Museum and Brent R. Benjamin and David Conradsen, we offer our gratitude for their kind loans of works by Czeschka.

We would also like to acknowledge the efforts of colleagues and associates of the DMA, without whom the research, conservation, exhibition, and publications surrounding the Wittgenstein Vitrine would not have been possible. These individuals and institutions include Ubaldo Vitali, Alton Bowman, and Kim Crozier, conservators in private practice; Pamela Hatchfield, Head of Objects Conservation, Museum of Fine Arts, Boston; Bruno Pouliot, Senior Conservator of Objects, Winterthur; Mark Popisil, Acting Curator of Minerals, Perot Museum of Nature and Science; Dr. Marcy Brown Marsden, Associate Dean, Constantin College, University of Dallas; Paul Asenbaum, Vienna; Benjamin Macklowe, president, Macklowe Gallery, New York City; Goppion, Milan; Flickinger Glassworks, Brooklyn; and Quin Mathews and Manny Alcala, Quin Mathews Films, Dallas. The conservation and casework for the vitrine were generously supported by an Art Conservation Project Grant from Bank of America.

Lastly, but most vitally, we extend our deepest appreciation to Margaret McDermott and the Trustees of The Eugene and Margaret McDermott Art Fund, Inc. for their extraordinary support and generosity in acquiring the vitrine both for the DMA and for generations of its visitors who now may marvel at this equally extraordinary masterwork of early twentieth-century design.

Maxwell L. Anderson
THE EUGENE MCDERMOTT DIRECTOR, DALLAS MUSEUM OF ART

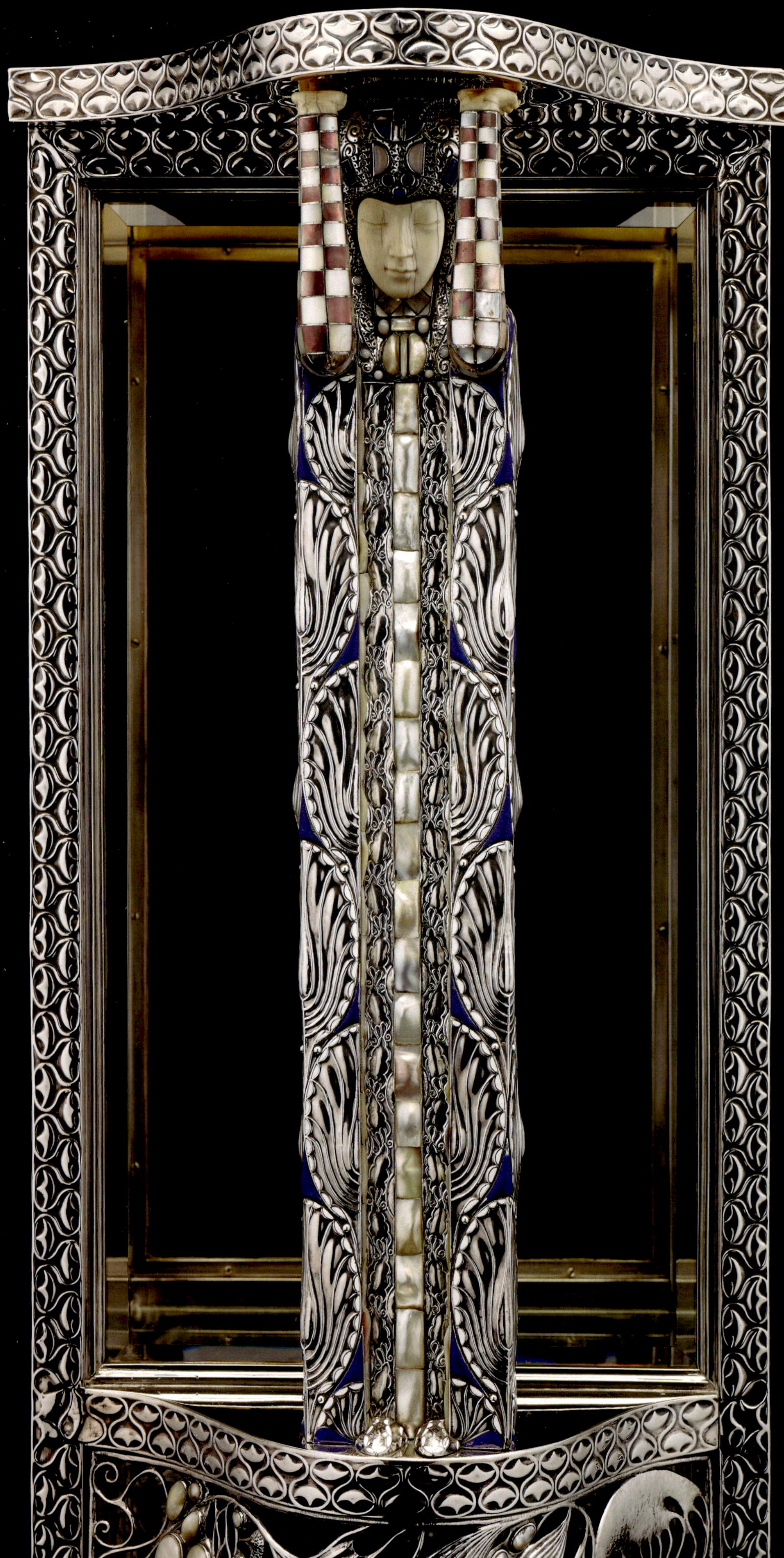

INTRODUCTION

ELISABETH SCHMUTTERMEIER

A true monument of invention, love, and taste

With these words the writer and journalist Ludwig Hevesi characterized Carl Otto Czeschka's vitrine in his review of the Vienna Kunstschau (art show) in 1908.[1] The exhibition had been initiated by a group around the painter Gustav Klimt and the architect Josef Hoffmann to coincide with the jubilee festivities in celebration of the sixty-year reign of Emperor Franz Josef. It was meant to call attention to contemporary Austrian art, including applied art and architecture, and give the Wiener Werkstätte an opportunity "to display its abilities for once to a broader public."[2] In was in this prestigious context that Czeschka's sumptuous vitrine was first presented in public.

The temporary exhibition hall was designed by Hoffmann, and he had envisioned a rectangular gallery (Room 50) specifically for the Wiener Werkstätte. Recessed into one of the room's long walls were five tall display cases in which selected works by the collective stood on inlaid shelves. On the opposite side, corresponding to the wall cases, were five tall windows. The room radiated an imposing harmony and unity, especially as the center of the space was unobstructed—except by the vitrine. According to the exhibition catalogue, the wall cases displayed "objects of applied art."[3] The center case held works by Czeschka,[4] and between this center case and the opposite window were the two objects by Czeschka that were distinguished by their association with their owners: the vitrine, already acquired by Karl Wittgenstein, and a casket that had been presented by Emil von Skoda to Emperor Franz Josef in 1906 as a souvenir of his visit to the Skoda Iron Works in Pilsen in 1905.[5] The elaborate vitrine was thus directly associated with, and shared the luster of, an object considered worthy of being a gift to the emperor. The vitrine, which had been initiated by the directors of the Wiener Werkstätte a long time before with an eye to an eventual public viewing, had been purchased by Karl Wittgenstein during the show.[6] Serving as a kind of advertisement, it was intended to display to a broader public the Wiener Werkstätte's masterly craftsmanship and motivate people to purchase one piece or another.[7] The singular value of the cabinet, the most expensive object the Wiener Werkstätte had ever produced, was also recognized by its buyer, for he placed it, together with other works of art, in the Red Salon of his residence, the Palais Wittgenstein, on Alleegasse. As a type of furniture, the vitrine goes back to the beginning of the nineteenth century. Thus, this particular vitrine, the overall concept of which may have been developed by Hoffmann—his monogram appears on the piece—was not a modern innovation;[8] it was the decoration by Czeschka that was contemporary.

In 1903 and 1904, when Hoffmann and Koloman Moser were the sole designers for the Wiener Werkstätte, the decoration of their mainly three-dimensional objects was quite restrained and, in some pieces of furniture, almost nonexistent. A few, mostly rectilinear, ornaments were placed on the walls of geometric vessels or on book bindings. By contrast, the jewelry designs by Moser and Hoffmann were dominated by curving lines and more or less highly stylized motifs from nature, such as fish, birds, pea pods, or leaves. Exquisite effects were achieved by the combination of flat shapes in silver or gold, either with designs of vegetation or unornamented, with projecting gemstones.

Czeschka, who joined the Werkstätte collective as a third designer in 1905, tended toward a more playful, more decorative style, one that increasingly covered ornamental pieces and tableware with stylized plant, fruit, or animal motifs placed close together. Over the course of his tenure at the Wiener Werkstätte, Czeschka abandoned stylization in favor of a greater naturalism, thus anticipating a trend in one of the variants of Viennese modernism. The special charm of his dazzling vitrine lies in its juxtaposition of the simplification and imitation of nature as clearly seen in the figures—their clothing and faces—and in the fretwork ornaments placed in front of the glass. Further interest was provided by the contrast between empty planes and busy ones and by the use of precious materials. The motif of grapevines with leaves and birds, seen in the fretwork, is also found in other designs by Czeschka, such as collar necklaces, lidded goblets, and centerpieces.

Hoffmann's work for the Wiener Werkstätte from this time—Moser left the collective in 1907—already exhibits increasingly naturalistic motifs as well, such as the oval or heart-shaped leaves, bellflowers, and vines seen on the textile arts of his Bohemian homeland, a heritage shared with Czeschka. The increased adoption of vegetable and zoomorphic motifs in the Wiener Werkstätte's ornamental repertoire as initiated by Czeschka found its artistic culmination in the work of Dagobert Peche. By introducing suggestions from abroad and thanks to his knowledge of and appreciation for period styles from the past, Peche furthered a new stylistic phase within the collective, designing representational, mostly stylized, plant motifs such as lancet-shaped or slender, elongated leaves, which he placed on precious objects in combination with grapes, truncated branches, floral bouquets, or geometric shapes.

The design of surfaces by the artists of the Wiener Werkstätte and their predilection for perfectly executed, exquisitely shaped objects in precious materials exhibited many of the features that would be found again in European and American Art Deco of the 1920s and 1930s. Czeschka's vitrine, with its combination of silver, semiprecious stones, ivory, mother-of-pearl, onyx, and Macassar ebony, anticipates the composition of some of the most luxurious furnishings of French Art Deco. The quest in these decades—and by other later designers—for new forms of expression that invoked tradition and history without relying on mere historicism found inspiration in the objects of the Wiener Werkstätte.

NOTES

1 Ludwig Hevesi, "Kunstschau 1908," *Kunst und Kunsthandwerk: Monatsschrift des k.k. Österreichisches Museum für Kunst und Industrie* 11 (1908), p. 396.

2 Berta Zuckerkandl, "Die Ausstellung der Klimt-Gruppe," *Wiener Allgemeine Zeitung,* November 2, 1907, p. 7.

3 In Case 1 were pieces by Otto Prutscher; in Case 2, works by Moser. Case 3 was devoted to Czeschka and, to a lesser degree, Karl Witzmann. Case 4 contained works by Hoffmann and Case 5 ceramics by Berthold Löffler and Michael Powolny; see Elisabeth Schmuttermeier, "Die Wiener Werkstätte auf der Kunstschau 1908," in *Gustav Klimt und die Kunstschau 1908,* ed. Agnes Husslein-Arco and Alfred Weidinger, exh. cat. Belvedere, Vienna (Munich: Prestel Verlag 2008), pp. 434–41.

4 These were works of applied art in silver, pieces of jewelry, wooden caskets with inlays and carvings in wood, ivory, and mother-of-pearl, a leather casket, and fans with hand-painted decorations on swan skin or silk. Visible inside the vitrine were two table centerpieces that are now in the collection of the Austrian Museum of Applied Arts (the MAK), Vienna, as well as a jardiniere of an unusual design and a tea service with samovar from the collection of Dr. Albert Figdor.

5 Emperor Franz Josef had visited the plant on September 9, 1905. The casket, which is now in the collection of the Austrian National Library, Vienna, contains a series of fifty-two photographs of the Skoda Works by Antonin Duras. It was created by the Wiener Werkstätte after a design by Carl Otto Czeschka in January 1906.

6 According to the entry in the Wiener Werkstätte's model book (this was Model No. S 1000, listed in Model Book 9, p. 1000 [archive of the Wiener Werkstätte, Austrian Museum of Applied Arts, Vienna]), several different craftsmen were employed in its creation. Their respective wages and hours are listed. According to an unpublished letter from Fritz Waerndorfer to Czeschka, dated June 5, 1908, Karl Wittgenstein paid thirty thousand crowns, of which two thousand were set aside as an honorarium for Czeschka, twenty-five thousand went to the Wiener Werkstätte, and the remaining three thousand to the Kunstschau.

7 On the initiative of the Ministry of Public Works, the Imperial Royal Austrian Museum for Art and Industry was authorized to purchase "modern art objects exhibited in the Kunstschau." The museum acquired more than twenty of the works on display.

8 Another far simpler vitrine, based on a design by Hoffmann, is in the possession of Wittgenstein descendants to this day: Model No. M 478, listed in Model Book 30, p. 478, dated January 29, 1906 (archive of the Wiener Werkstätte, Austrian Museum of Applied Arts, Vienna).

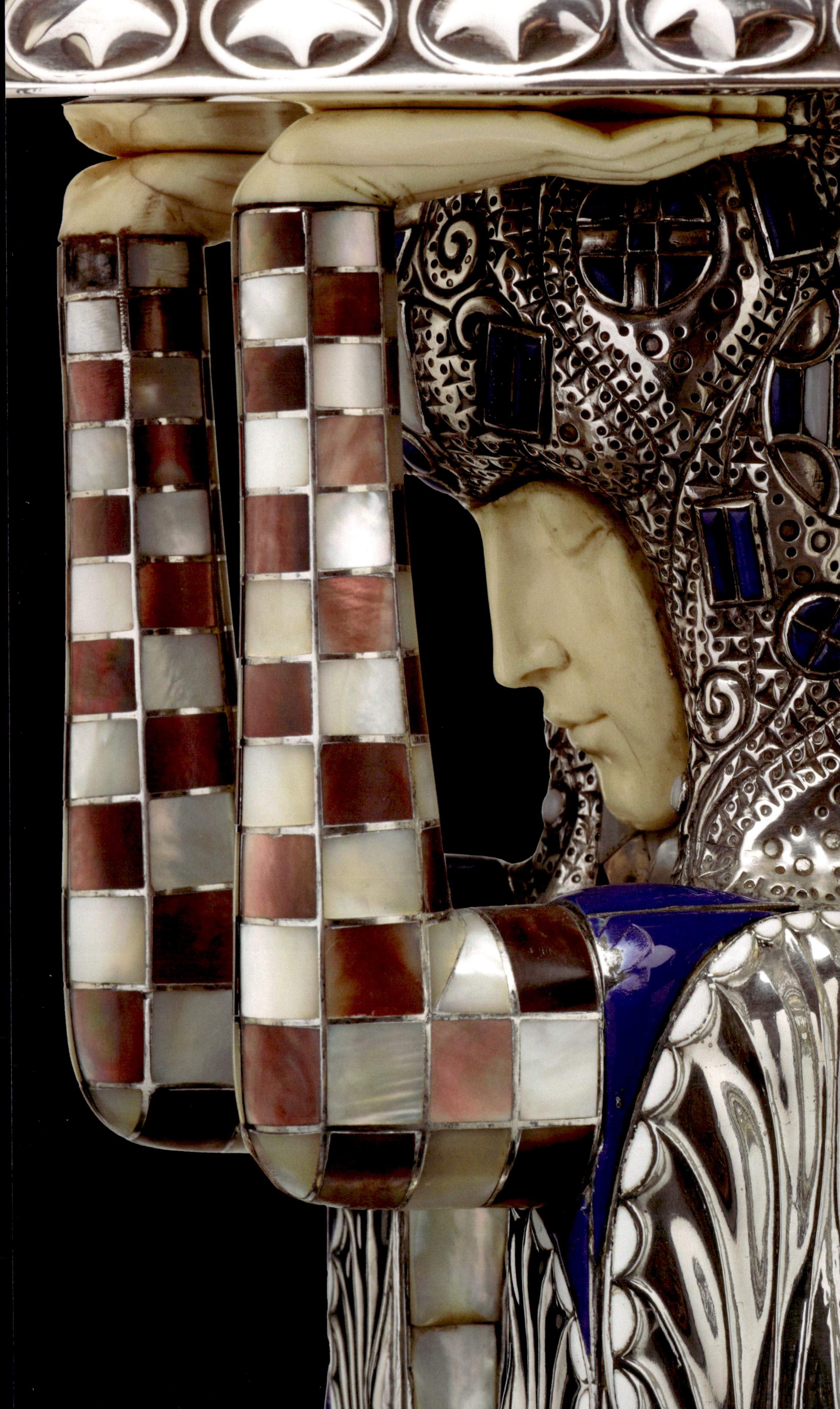

THE WITTGENSTEIN VITRINE
MODERN OPULENCE IN VIENNA

KEVIN W. TUCKER

At the Kunstschau exhibition two years ago ample opportunity was offered to see how great an artist Czeschka is. One object shown there will alone assure his name going down to posterity—a magnificent silver cabinet . . .

—Amelia Sarah Levetus, 1911

In 1908, the designer Carl Otto Czeschka (1878–1960) revealed to Vienna the most lavish creation of the Wiener Werkstätte, a vitrine of solid silver, decorated with twin sculptural figures and woodland creatures, all encrusted with gemstones and set atop an ebony socle or base. Appearing at that year's Vienna Kunstschau (art show) in a gallery dedicated to the creations of the Werkstätte, a collective of artists, designers, and craftspeople, Czeschka's great glass and silver cabinet served as the centerpiece of the activities of the collective in fashioning stylish, luxurious goods for Austria's cultural elite. Far more than a mere showcase for other objects, the vitrine stood alone in the center of the room and, with its richly decorative motifs and opulent materials, marked the tensions inherent in the artistic and financial goals of the Werkstätte and the Arts and Crafts guilds from which its ideology sprang. Czeschka's vitrine stood at the intersection of aesthetic, cultural, and political shifts in the early twentieth century and could be cast by critics then, as now, as either a retardataire fragment of a rapidly fading Gilded Age or as a herald of one branch of the early twentieth-century progressive movements that sought to consider how modernity should be represented as either an ideology or a style. Few objects capture the conflicted ambitions of international designers and the *Zeitgeist* of Vienna in the first decade of the new century as effectively as does this work.[1]

It may in part be due to this tension and the narrow arc of Modernism, with its reductivist, functionalist, and optimistically democratic ideologies, that Czeschka's own legacy has often been overshadowed by the careers of his better-known peers, among them, the architect

Josef Hoffmann and the artist Koloman Moser. Czeschka's official association with the organization began after it was founded, and he himself remained in Vienna only until 1907, but his contract work continued until World War I and amounted to a significant volume of designs.[2] His relatively brief tenure as a participant in Vienna, together with the fact that his work tended to include a larger proportion of graphic arts, including postcard illustrations and textile design, probably contributed to the perception that Czeschka was only one of a stable of designers, a perception that may have solidified in the ensuing years as other artists joined the collective. That his designs were absorbed within the overall identity of the organization or occasionally seen (whether accurately or not) as a decorative component of some of Hoffmann's own works, are yet other considerations. However lauded and well regarded he was at the time, his contemporaries perceived him primarily as a graphic and *decorative* artist, his talents tending toward expressive ornamentation rather than toward considerations of form and function.

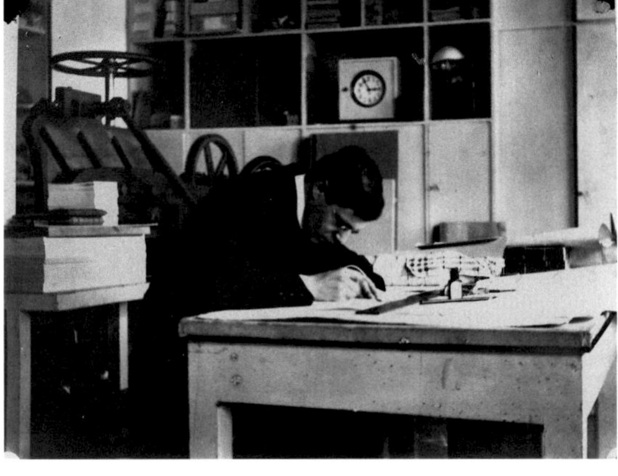

FIGURE 1 Carl Otto Czeschka in the Wiener Werkstätte bookbinding studio, Vienna, c. 1906. MAK: Austrian Museum of Applied Arts/ Contemporary Art, Vienna (WWF 137-3-1).

Of Moravian-Bohemian ancestry, Carl Otto Czeschka (fig. 1) was born in Vienna in 1878 to Matilde and Wenceslaus Czeschka, a seamstress and woodworker, respectively. Out of personal interest, he began to frequent the library of the Österreichischen Museums für Kunst und Industrie (the Austrian Museum of Applied Arts, now the MAK) in 1889 and, in 1891, he studied art in evening classes, his training supported through tutoring the children of Archduke Karl Ludwig—a post facilitated by the artist Koloman Moser.[3] In 1894 Czeschka entered the Akademie der bildenden Künste Wien (the Vienna Academy of Fine Arts) and began studying under Christian Griepenkerl. Following a series of travels in 1897 and 1898, Czeschka began his independent career in earnest by producing, alongside those of his mentor and colleague Moser, allegorical and other illustrations in the *Jugendstil* fashion for Gerlach and Schenk, a Viennese publisher.[4] Soon thereafter, he joined the Vienna Secession, the group of artists led by Gustav Klimt who, in 1897, had repudiated the conventions of the Union of Austrian Artists to establish their own body.[5] Czeschka's association was reflected in his taking up the motifs and stylings that the Secessionists favored at the turn of the twentieth century. Nationalistic themes, the sinuous lines of *Jugendstil* design, and Czeschka's own predilection for the stylized, organic pattern work that would come to characterize his subsequent career with the Werkstätte began to occur with regularity in the drawings and prints he produced.

In 1902, Czeschka participated in the Secession's fourteenth exhibition, which honored Ludwig van Beethoven, and he began teaching drawing classes, part time, at Vienna's Kunstgewerbeschule (School of Applied Arts). Acquainted years earlier with Koloman Moser, who was also a member of the Vienna Secession, Czeschka began collaborating with him and Rudolf von Larisch on the designs of publications to commemorate the hundredth anniversary of the Österreichische Staatsdruckerei (Austrian State Printers).[6] Increasingly, Czeschka became recognized as a talented graphic designer, and his distinctive illustrative style would soon come to shape every aspect of his designs for other media, including textiles, metalwork, jewelry, stained glass, interior design, and furnishings.

THE WIENER WERKSTÄTTE

The formation of the Wiener Werkstätte in 1903 by Josef Hoffmann and Koloman Moser with the support of their patron, the industrialist Fritz Waerndorfer, would have a decided effect on both Czeschka's career and, through the international attention given to the organization's efforts, the identity of early twentieth-century progressive design. The manifesto promulgated by Moser and Hoffmann in the *Arbeitsprogramm* (work program) of the association provides an insight into their goals and principles in organizing the new group:

> *We wish to create an inner relationship linking public, designer, and worker, and we want to produce good and simple articles of everyday use. Our guiding principle is function; utility our first condition, and our strength must lie in good proportions and the proper treatment of material. We shall seek to decorate when it seems required but we do not feel obligated to adorn at any price. We shall use many semi-precious stones, especially in our jewelry, because in our eyes their manifold colors and ever-varying facets replace the sparkle of diamonds. We love silver and gold for their sheen and regard the luster of copper just as valid artistically.*[7]

Despite these democratic sensibilities, the artists found that the realities of high cost and limited clientele for such progressive designs created an inherent conflict between the refined, handmade objects they produced and their ability to engage a sufficient number of customers who would seek out objects made of common materials used in a restrained manner, but which were, nonetheless, far more expensive than their mass-produced counterparts. The manifesto affirms the genesis of the Werkstätte in the philosophy of the English Arts and Crafts movement, particularly the work of Charles Robert Ashbee's Guild of the Handicraft, but as the scholar Christian Witt-Dörring has noted, "there was a clear hierarchy at the Wiener Werkstätte that subordinated artisans to artists." In the organization, artisans were rarely encouraged to become artists or designers and the artists rarely worked as artisans; the sociopolitical reform of the Arts and Crafts movement cited by the Werkstätte was "scarcely observed in actual practice."[8] The artist or designer as creator remained paramount, and the symbolically democratizing principles of favoring base metals and semiprecious stones over precious jewels seems to have been irrelevant in the creation of what were artistic, but largely expensive, luxury objects.

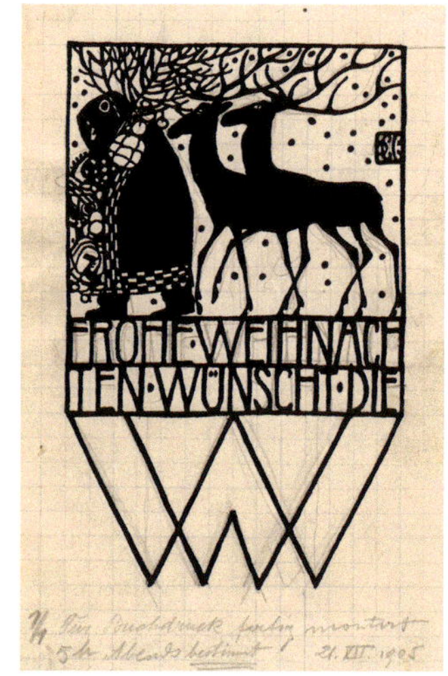

FIGURE 2 Among the first postcards produced by the Wiener Werkstätte was a Christmas card for 1905, designed by Czeschka and identified by his mark as well as the group's "WW" logo. A preliminary study is reproduced above. MAK: Austrian Museum of Applied Arts/Contemporary Art, Vienna (KI 11585).

The concomitant notion of a *Gesamtkunstwerk,* or total work of art in which the architecture, furnishings, and even the attire of the occupants might be designed as a harmonious whole, only reinforced the exclusive nature of their work. Ultimately, their ability to produce even relatively inexpensive independent articles, such as artistic postcards (fig. 2)—among Czeschka's first documented creations, in December of 1905, as a member of the Werkstätte—would depend not only upon substantial commissions but also on the continuing favor of their elite patrons, such as Waerndorfer and the wealthy Viennese industrialist Karl Wittgenstein (1847–1913, fig. 3), among others. Its precarious financial structure and inability to recoup production expenses would plague the organization and contribute to the departure of its cofounder, Moser, by 1907. Nevertheless, the Werkstätte expanded and remained in operation until 1932, but it struggled constantly with the challenges of shifting tastes and the parlous financing that is inherent in an organization intent on upholding high craft and design standards for artistic goods that were both preferred by and affordable for the relatively few patrons who were both wealthy and culturally progressive.

FLIGHTS OF FANCY

By the time his association with the Werkstätte became official in September of 1905, the three basic motifs of Czeschka's ornamental scheme for the vitrine had already been suggested by parallels in his other designs and those of his Viennese peers—sinuous vines with leaves,

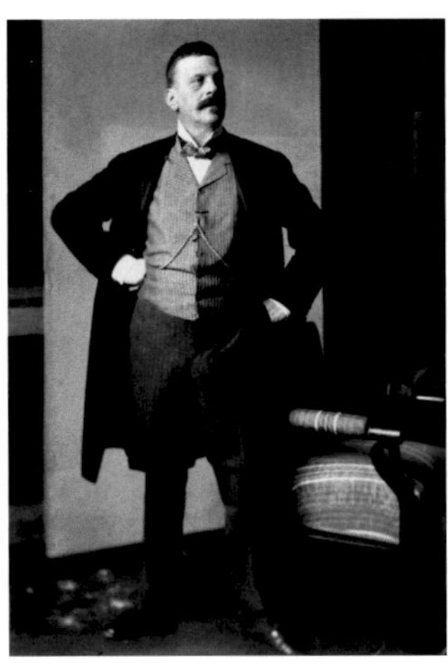

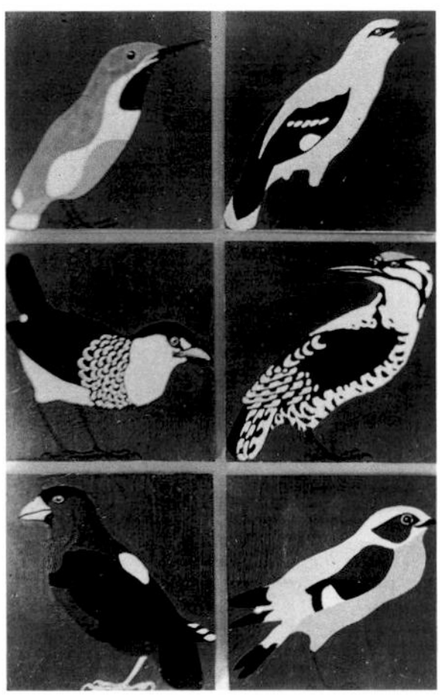

armored knights, and elegantly stylized birds and other animals. The latter motif was used extensively and may be seen to particular effect in his work with Josef Hoffmann, Koloman Moser, Richard Luksch, and Elena Luksch-Makowsky for Wittgenstein's hunting lodge at Hochreith, Austria. Within Hoffmann's grid of polished wood wall coverings, Czeschka set enameled images of single birds (fig. 4) as well as groups of birds nesting within baskets of flowers. For Hoffmann's oak chairs to be used at a games table (fig. 5), he designed upholstery with motifs including a doe and round-headed flower (figs. 6 and 7), suggesting the influence of the textiles of his own Moravian ancestry and evoking the rustic setting and purpose of the hunting lodge. A repoussé panel, mounted above a doorway, that depicts a classicized nude hunter on horseback, with bow and arrows, amidst a field of stylized flowers and birds (fig. 8), further reinforces the overall scheme; the hunter's prey, a stag, served as the logo (also designed by Czeschka) for the lodge. In a contemporary review of the Hochreith lodge rooms, Czeschka was cited as the "ornamentalist" of the group, noted for his "fantastic playfulness" and work that testified to the "delicacy of his artistic feelings."[9] Moser had already incorporated fanciful bird and animal graphic designs in his own work, notably within an elongated female form on a poster that was used for various purposes, including a Russian advertisement for the furniture manufacturer J. & J. Kohn (fig. 9). The similarities to Czeschka's design for the pierced silver panels of the vitrine are remarkable: squirrels and birds perch on curling vines or branches adjacent to flowers and small clusters suggestive of fruit. Unlike the silhouettes used in Moser's poster, Czeschka's designs for painted birds at Hochreith—and later, those fashioned in silver for the vitrine—would provide a level of detail sufficient to distinguish the species.

FIGURE 3 Photograph of Karl Wittgenstein, 1908. Österreichische Nationalbibliothek, Vienna.

FIGURE 4 Enameled wall plaques of birds designed for Karl Wittgenstein's hunting lodge in Hochreith, Austria, c. 1906. Archival photograph, MAK: Austrian Museum of Applied Arts/Contemporary Art, Vienna (WWF 105-280-2).

The bird motif (figs. 10 and 11) was not limited to commissions for Wittgenstein, nor would it be confined to the rural setting of a hunting lodge. Another Czeschka collaboration, a tall-case clock (figs. 12 and 13)

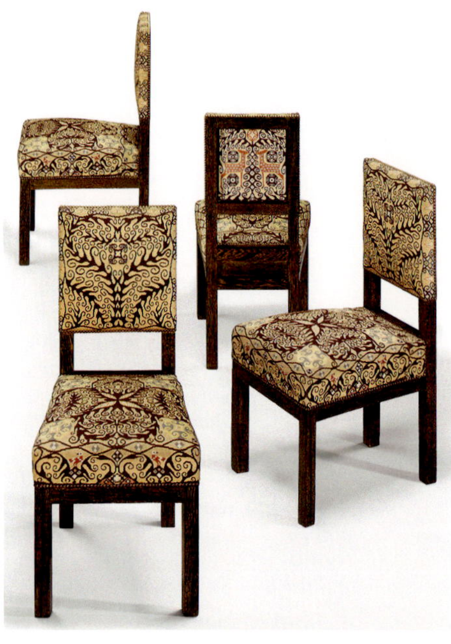

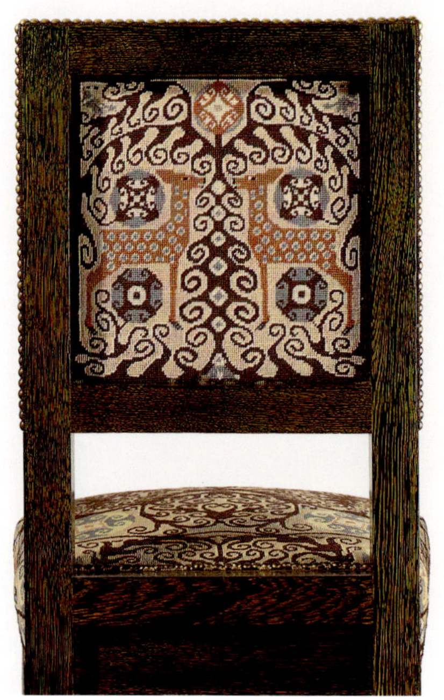

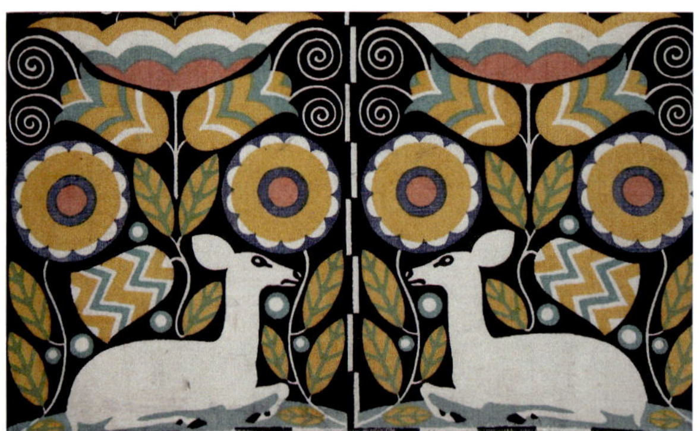

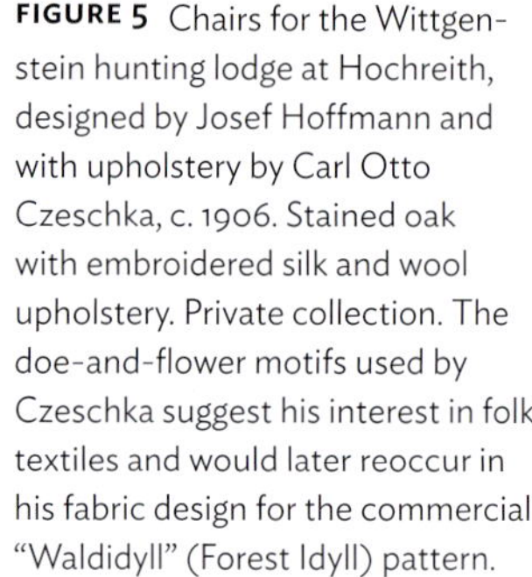

FIGURE 5 Chairs for the Wittgenstein hunting lodge at Hochreith, designed by Josef Hoffmann and with upholstery by Carl Otto Czeschka, c. 1906. Stained oak with embroidered silk and wool upholstery. Private collection. The doe-and-flower motifs used by Czeschka suggest his interest in folk textiles and would later reoccur in his fabric design for the commercial "Waldidyll" (Forest Idyll) pattern.

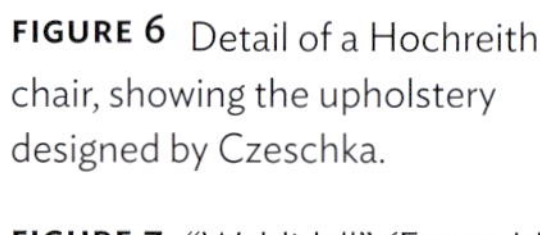

FIGURE 6 Detail of a Hochreith chair, showing the upholstery designed by Czeschka.

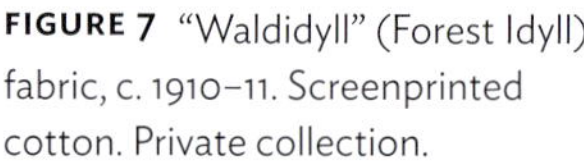

FIGURE 7 "Waldidyll" (Forest Idyll) fabric, c. 1910–11. Screenprinted cotton. Private collection.

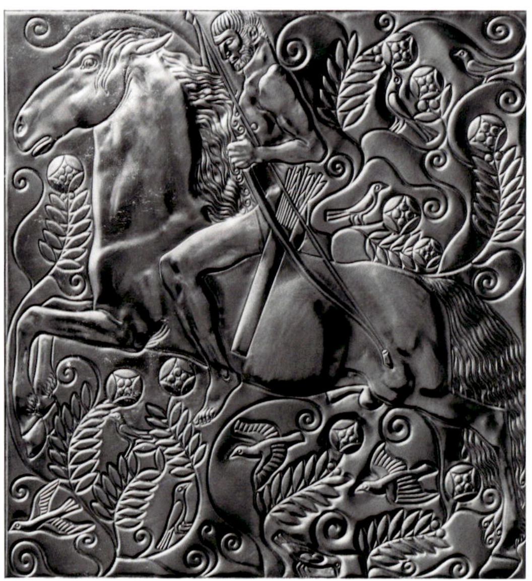

FIGURE 8 Repoussé overdoor panel of hunter with birds and flowers, designed for the Wittgenstein hunting lodge at Hochreith, c. 1906. Archival photograph, MAK: Austrian Museum of Applied Arts/Contemporary Art, Vienna (WWF 103-136-1).

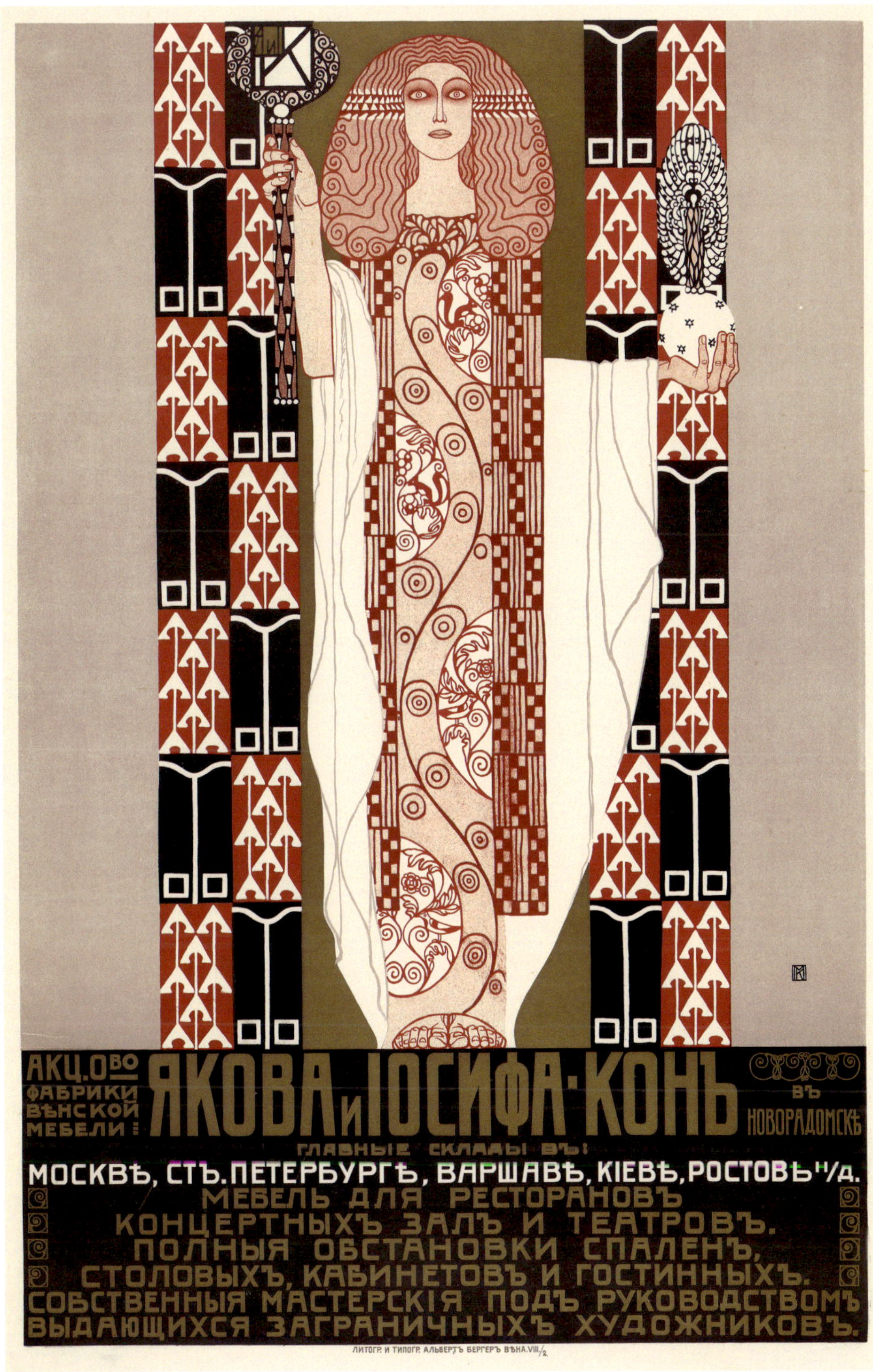

FIGURE 9 Koloman Moser, poster for J. & J. Kohn (for the Russian market), 1904. Colored lithograph on paper. Wien Museum.

made for an unknown client, exhibits a simplified repoussé bird and vine motif set within the framework of Hoffmann's highly architectonic case.[10] Even so, whether by their patron's preference or Czeschka's own inclination for a leitmotif of nature that is often affiliated with the Arts and Crafts iconography of a Tree of Life or the regenerative power of Spring, a similar theme would be repeated in both the vitrine and yet another work acquired by Wittgenstein, a fire screen sited in the Red Salon in the family's mansion, the Palais Wittgenstein on Vienna's Alleegasse. This fire screen (fig. 14), which was placed across the room from the vitrine, had a giltwood frame designed by Hoffmann for a textile designed by Czeschka and characterized by birds, leaves, and elaborated versions of the abstracted floral roundels used in the repoussé panel at Hochreith, together with motifs to be found in a host of his works in other media, notably his program cover and a costume design for the Cabaret Fledermaus in 1907 (figs. 15 and 16). For the vitrine, these roundels or flower heads appear, transformed, in the enameled cruciform medallions decorating the silver coifs of the twin figures that flank the case (fig. 17).

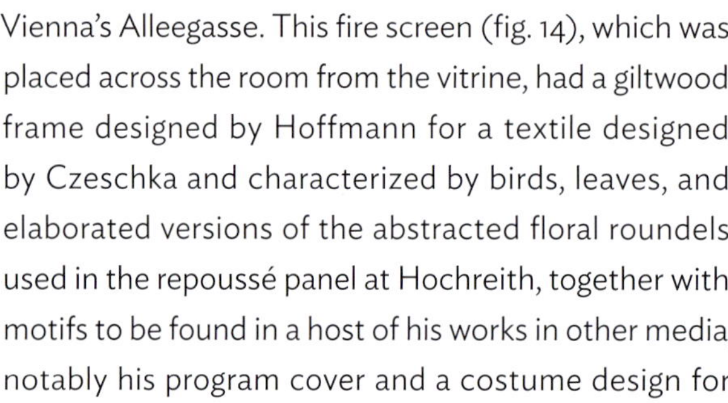

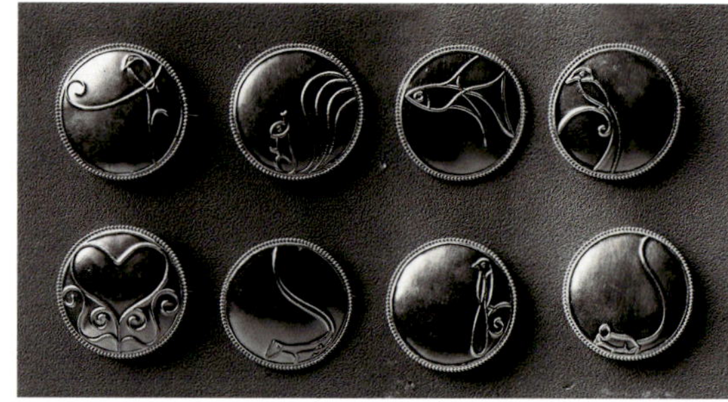

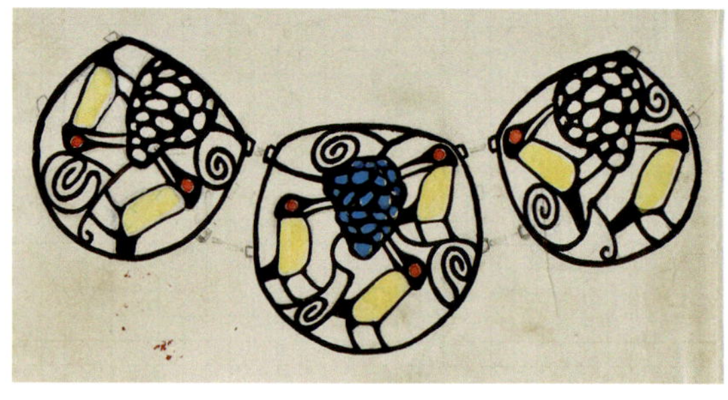

FIGURE 10 Hat-pin tops and brooches with animal designs, 1906. MAK: Austrian Museum of Applied Arts/Contemporary Art, Vienna (WWF 91-33-1).

FIGURE 11 Necklace design with birds and berries, c. 1905. Pencil and gouache on paper. MAK: Austrian Museum of Applied Arts/Contemporary Art, Vienna (WWE 72-1).

THE KNIGHT

In the late 1890s Czeschka's drawings began to reflect his interest in imagery that recalled medievalist pageant and chivalry, particularly the theme of the heroic knight with its nationalistic cultural associations glorifying the heritage of the political structure of imperial Europe. Beginning with his travels to Wörthersee and Passau in 1897, Czeschka's sketches included a variety of medieval Scandinavian and Central European motifs, including weapons, clothing, and other objects. His surviving studies from 1897 and 1898 include images of the armor of the Emperor Maximilian I, drawn during one of his many visits to Vienna's museums.[11] Scholars have noted his childhood interest in horses and the processions of the imperial cavalry in the emperor's spring parade.[12] Within the context of the

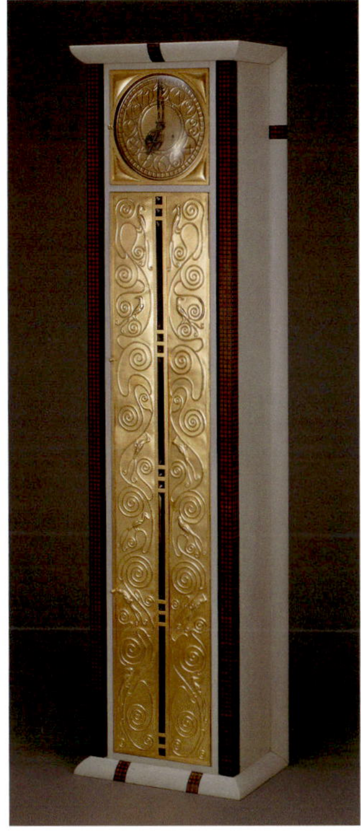

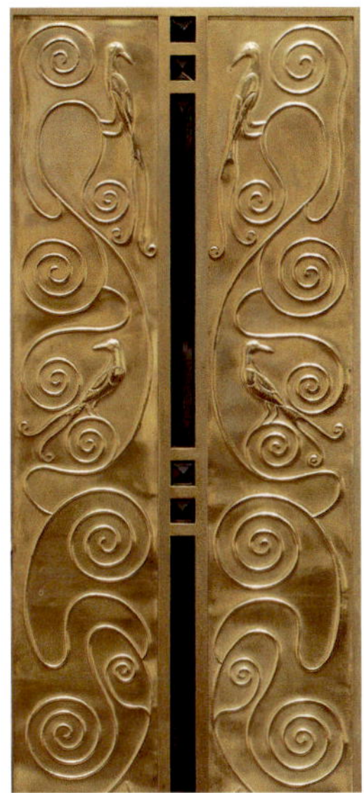

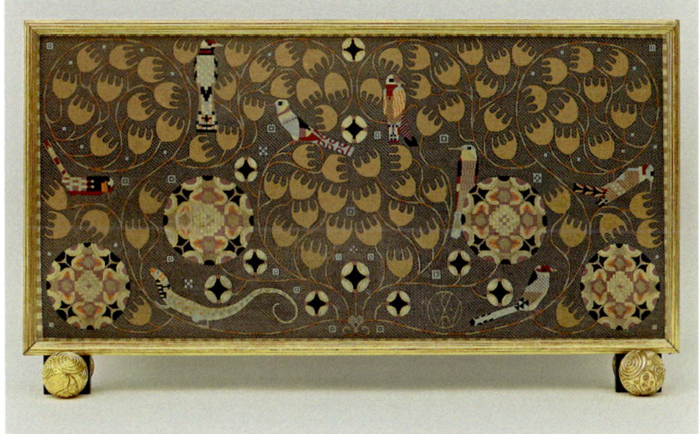

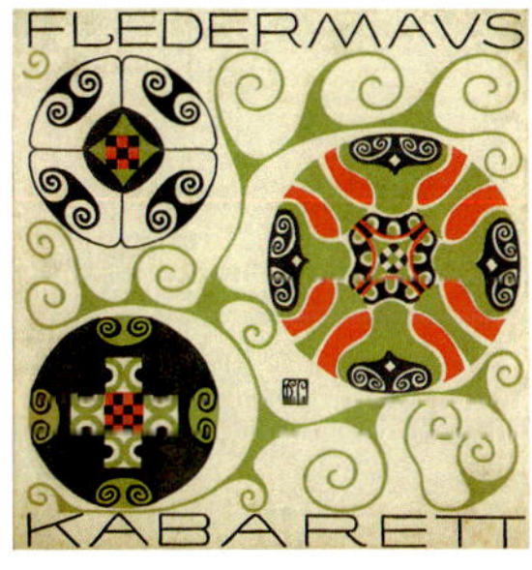

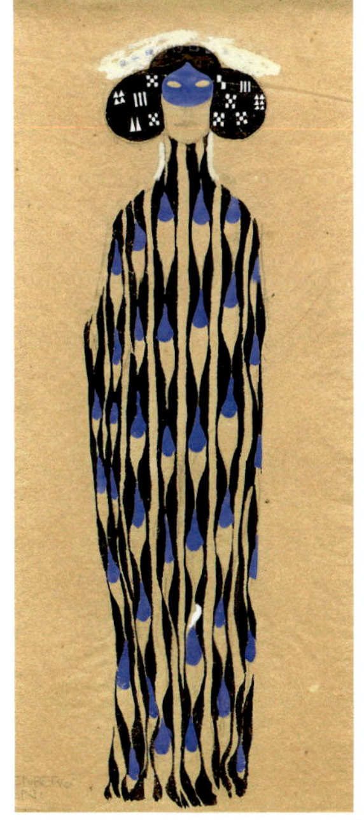

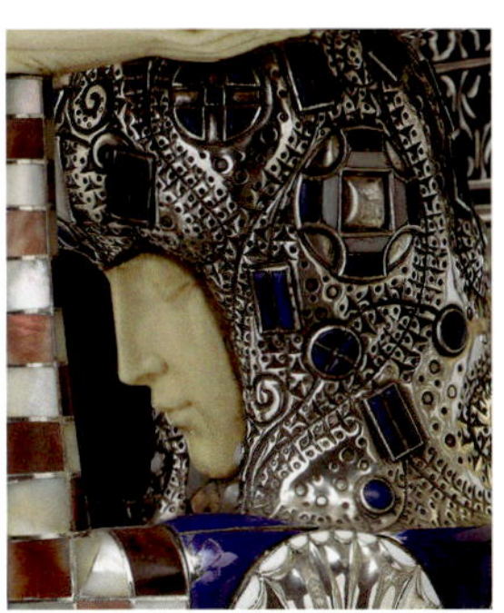

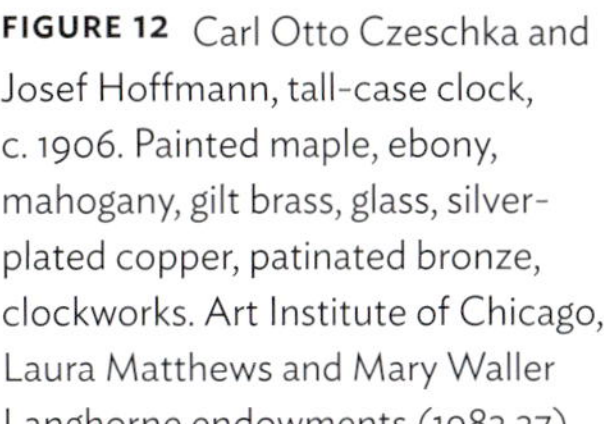

FIGURE 12 Carl Otto Czeschka and Josef Hoffmann, tall-case clock, c. 1906. Painted maple, ebony, mahogany, gilt brass, glass, silver-plated copper, patinated bronze, clockworks. Art Institute of Chicago, Laura Matthews and Mary Waller Langhorne endowments (1983.37).

FIGURE 13 Detail of the tall-case clock showing Czeschka's repoussé bird-and-vine motif.

FIGURE 14 Fire screen with an embroidered bird-and-flower design by Czeschka set within a frame designed by Josef Hoffmann, c. 1906. Frame: oak stained black; textile: petit-point embroidery. MAK: Austrian Museum of Applied Arts/Contemporary Art, Vienna (T-12765).

FIGURE 15 Program cover, Cabaret Fledermaus, 1907. Color lithograph. IMAGNO/Austrian Archives.

FIGURE 16 Costume design, "Dark Mask," for the Cabaret Fledermaus, 1907. Theaterwissenschaftliche Sammlung, University of Cologne.

FIGURE 17 Vitrine, detail of one of the standing figures.

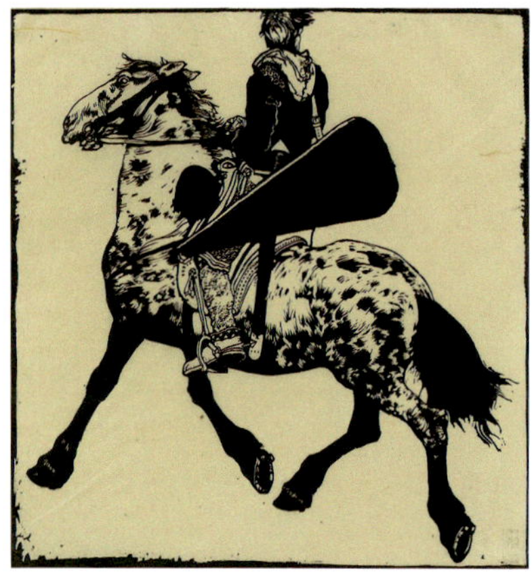

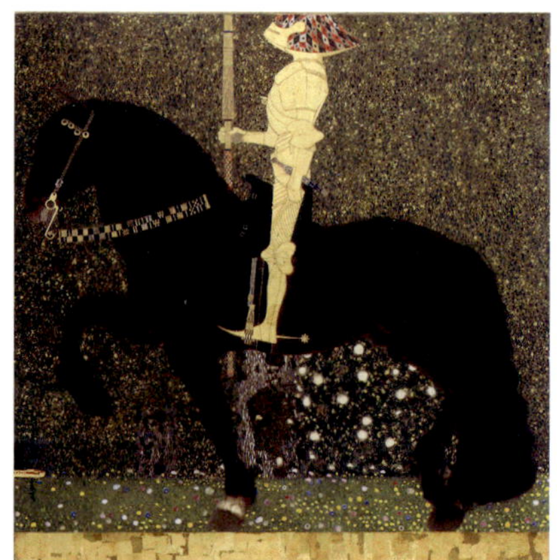

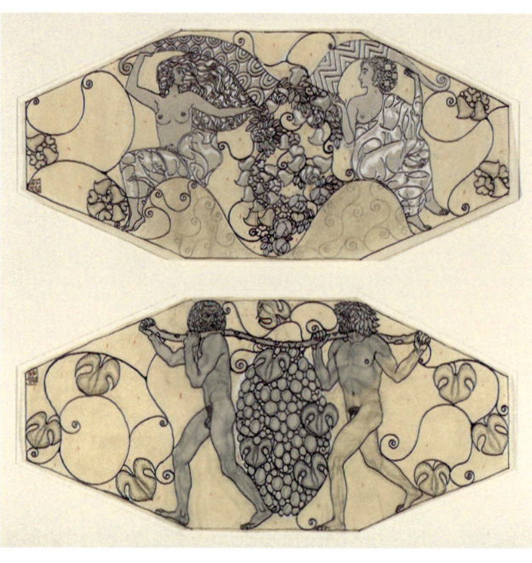

Austro-Hungarian empire and the nationalistic fervor gripping Europe at the turn of the century, such imagery permitted Czeschka to express his own romantic fantasy (fig. 18). As a representation of historic lineage, nobility, and power and akin to the Wagnerian ideal of the heroic savior, these themes were exploited as a motif by German and Austrian artists, including Klimt, who, in his Beethoven frieze of the 1902 Secession exhibition, consolidated them within an otherworldly narrative. Klimt continued the motif in the painting *Life Is a Struggle* or *The Golden Knight* of 1903 (fig. 19), a work subsequently acquired by Karl Wittgenstein and hung in the family mansion. Depicting the figure of the knight in profile on horseback, the painting may be considered, in light of its original title, as a cosmic struggle for happiness against the forces of the world; one may also consider it in the context of the earlier symbolist fashion for the figure of Saint George as "both a defender of the arts and conqueror of tyranny," allied to the image of the wealthy industrialist Wittgenstein himself and his efforts in supporting the arts, including the Secession and the Werkstätte.[13] Klimt's body of work undoubtedly resonated with Czeschka not only because the two artists were early members of the Secessionist group, but also because they both contributed to the Werkstätte's great commission in Brussels, the Palais Stoclet, where Klimt again returned to the theme of the knight and Czeschka's contributions included numerous decorative elements including the design of a bacchanalian bas-relief (fig. 20). This close association would

FIGURE 18 *The Rider,* c. 1902. Woodcut. Museum für Kunst und Gewerbe, Hamburg, gift of Mr. Henner Steinbrecht to the estate of C. O. Czeschka, 1974 (1975.48).

FIGURE 19 Gustav Klimt, *Das Leben ein Kampf (Life is a Struggle)* or *Der goldene Ritter (The Golden Knight),* 1903. Oil, tempera, and gold on canvas. Aichi Prefectural Museum of Art, Nagoya, Japan.

FIGURE 20 Designs for a bas-relief for the Palais Stoclet, Brussels, c. 1907. MAK: Austrian Museum of Applied Arts/Contemporary Art, Vienna (KI-10403).

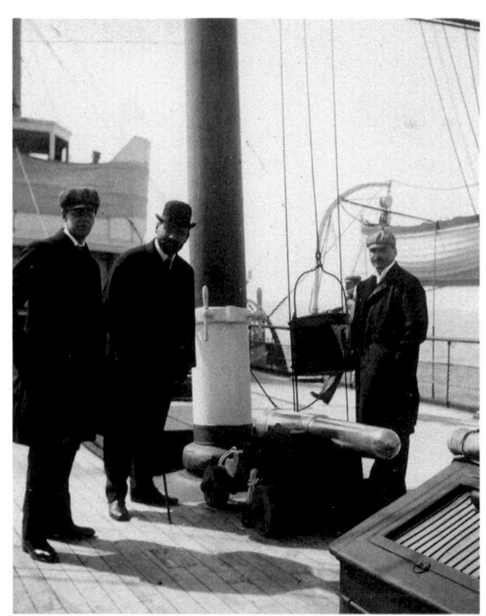

FIGURE 21 Carl Otto Czeschka (left), Gustav Klimt (center), and Fritz Waerndorfer (right), on a boat crossing the English Channel, May 1906. Photograph by Josef Hoffmann. Picture Library, Österreichische Nationalbibliothek, Vienna.

also afford Czeschka the opportunity to travel in May of 1906 with Klimt, Hoffmann, and Fritz Waerndorfer (fig. 21) to both Brussels (to review the Palais Stoclet construction site) and London, where he visited the Imperial Royal Austrian exhibition at Earl's Court and may have met with Charles Robert Ashbee, the founder of the Guild of the Handicraft and a source of inspiration for the creation of the Wiener Werkstätte.[14]

Czeschka's own designs for such chivalric figures began with his early studies of arms and armor and continued through the end of the decade. They included, in 1906 and 1907, carved and inset figures of the kings of the four suites on a card table (fig. 22), a box for Karl Wittgenstein (fig. 23), wooden toy knights (fig. 24), and set and costume designs for stage productions of *King Lear* by Max Reinhardt in Berlin and of *Die Nibelungen* by Friederich Hebbel in Vienna (fig. 25). The latter, while unrealized, would provide him with a vocabulary of designs for his most famous illustrated work, an edition of *Die Nibelungen,* published by Gerlach and Wiedling in 1909, in which brilliantly colored figures in bold geometric patterns dominated. In these images, Czeschka allied his aesthetic interests to a Wagnerian mythos to create fantastic scenes of warfare, heroes, and royal processions (figs. 26 and 27). In his final design for the vitrine, Czeschka adapted this imagery but without the context of any obvious narrative—two androgynous armored figures, each cloaked in a shimmering silver cape of patterned enamel designs, flank the cabinet as protective sentinels. Here, too, the symmetrical pairing suggests the influence of his colleagues, notably Moser, whose penchant for paired, attenuated figures can be seen in his armoire for Hans Eisler von Terramare (c. 1902–1903, Leopold Museum Collection, Vienna), a painted cupboard from 1905 (location unknown), and a silver box with flanking enamel panels of male figures (1906, MAK Collection, Vienna). However, Czeschka's figures are armored protectors (as indicated by their coifs, which look like chain mail). It has been suggested (in the context of the vitrine's other decorative motifs) that the figures also represent a spring awakening (*Frühlingserwachen*) that recalls a mystical relationship of all living beings in nature.[15] Interestingly, an extant photograph of carved and painted wood figures attributed to Czeschka (fig. 28) implies that an earlier iteration of the vitrine's sentinel caryatids may have been considered. Those figures, more

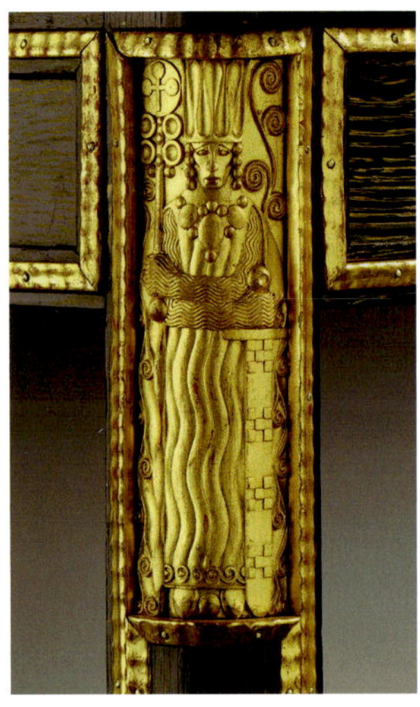

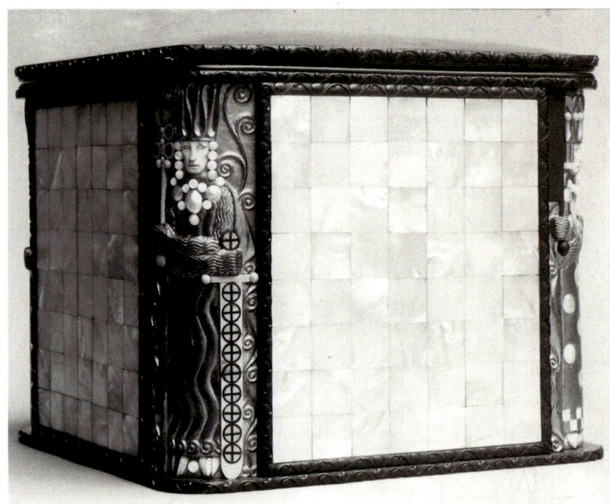

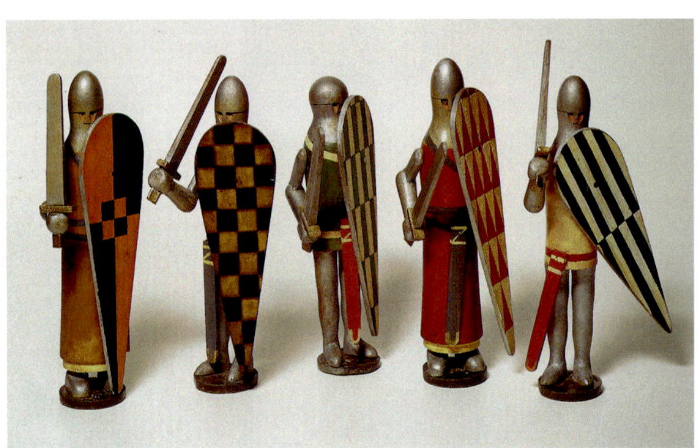

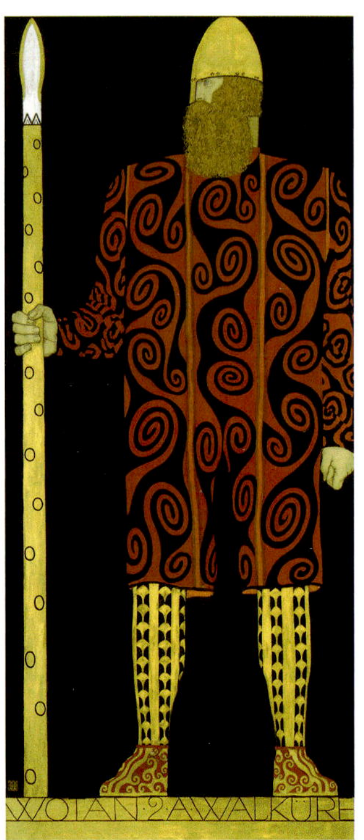

FIGURE 22 Games table for Karl Wittgenstein (detail), designed by Josef Hoffmann and with carved panels by Carl Otto Czeschka, c. 1907. Stained oak with carved and gilt lime wood. Private collection.

FIGURE 23 Card case for a games table with carved panels by Carl Otto Czeschka, c. 1907. Archival photograph, MAK: Austrian Museum of Applied Arts/Contemporary Art, Vienna (WWF 103-164-2).

FIGURE 24 Toy knights (*Nibelungen*), with moveable arms, c. 1908–10. Painted beechwood. Archival photograph, Galerie bei der Albertina, Vienna.

FIGURE 25 Design for Wotan's costume, exhibited at the Kunstschau, Vienna, 1908. MAK: Austrian Museum of Applied Arts/Contemporary Art, Vienna (LHG-185).

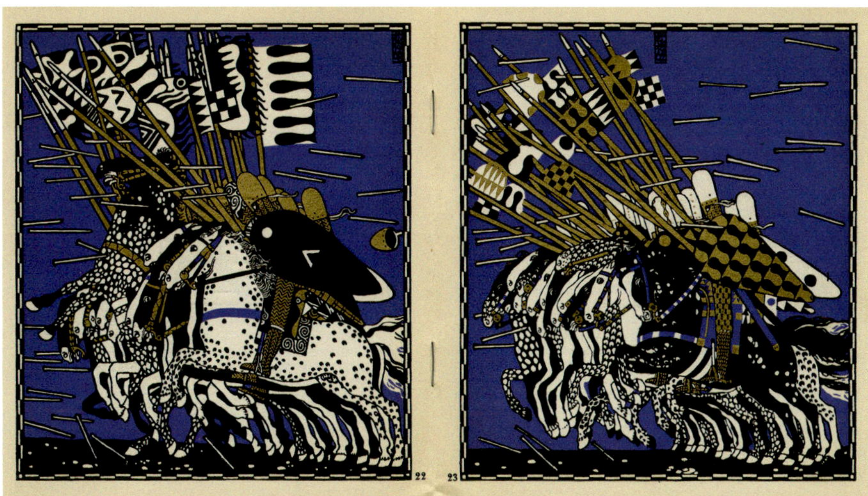

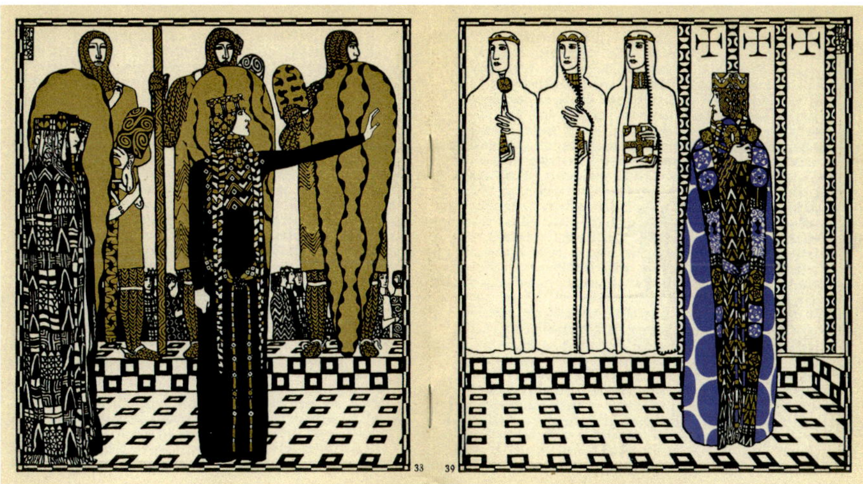

FIGURE 26 "Cavalry Charge," in Franz Keim, *Die Nibelungen,* illustrated by Czeschka and published by Gerlach and Wiedling (1909). Lithograph with gold. Dallas Museum of Art, gift of the Professional Members League (2014.35).

FIGURE 27 "The Quarrel of the Queens," in Franz Keim, *Die Nibelungen,* illustrated by Czeschka and published by Gerlach and Wiedling (1909). Lithograph with gold. Dallas Museum of Art, gift of the Professional Members League (2014.35).

FIGURE 28 Caryatid models, 1908. Archival photograph, MAK: Austrian Museum of Applied Arts/Contemporary Art, Vienna (WWF 105-268-1).

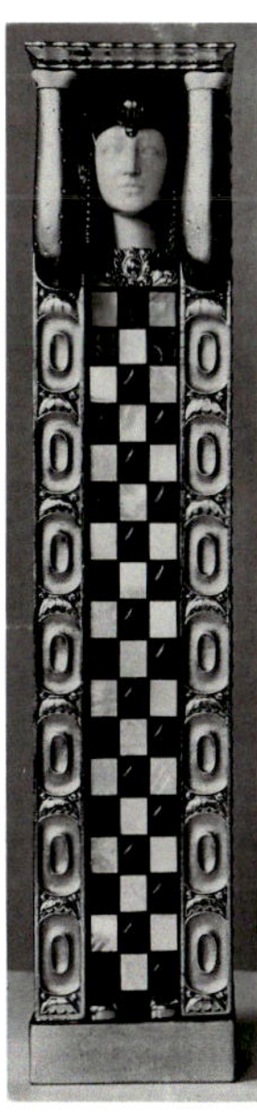

rectilinear in form and with hair styles after the antique, are similarly positioned with hands upraised, but the overall impression they convey is of an ancient Mediterranean past rather than the medievalist imagery Czeschka would perfect in his work for *Die Nibelungen.*[16]

THE VITRINE AND THE VIENNA KUNSTSCHAU

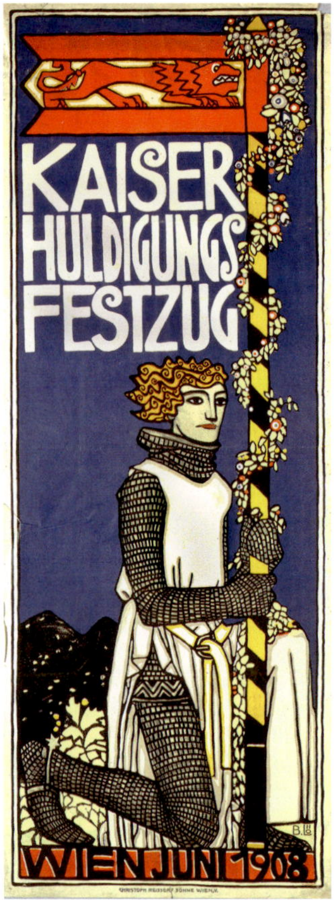

FIGURE 29 Berthold Löffler, poster for the Kunstschau, Vienna, 1908. Wien Museum.

The vitrine appeared in public for the first time in June of 1908 at that year's Kunstschau in Vienna which was a public exhibition organized for the jubilee honoring the sixty-year reign of the Austrian Emperor Franz Josef (fig. 29). More than 170 artists, including Klimt, Moser, Franz Metzner, and former students of Czeschka from the Vienna School of Applied Arts, Oskar Kokoschka and Berthold Löffler, took part, marking the rise of a new generation of progressive Viennese artists since Klimt and his followers left the Secession in 1905. Within an expansive pavilion designed by Hoffmann (fig. 30), the show featured artwork in a variety of media, including metal and ceramics, and assorted small articles made by the Werkstätte and displayed in a dedicated gallery. Czeschka's work was prominent. In one wall cabinet, a large silver jardiniere with mythical, satyr-like figures (fig. 31) was on display and, across from it, in its own display case near a window, a silver-gilt and ivory casket (the *Kaiserkassette,* fig. 32), which had been completed by the Werkstätte in early 1906. Commissioned by Emil von Skoda, a manufacturer of industrial components and armaments and a business associate of Karl Wittgenstein, the casket was presented to the emperor in honor of his visit to the Skoda Iron Works at Pilsen in September 1905.[17] But the vitrine was, as Fritz Waerndorfer, a co-founder of the Werkstätte, wrote to Czeschka, "our entire exhibition."[18] Within a protective glass case and alone in the center of the room stood Czeschka's great work (fig. 33):

> *The main piece is something unique; a silver vitrine by Czeschka. The work took two and a half years under "C's" supervision. Working on it, the artisans, foremost Mr. Erbrich, became specialists, as you become when exploring the temper, potential, and nature of an art work over the course of many years. Fifteen thousand crowns were spent creating this magnificent specimen that will be the highlight of the art show. It is of open-work ornament of leaves with fruit, grapes,*

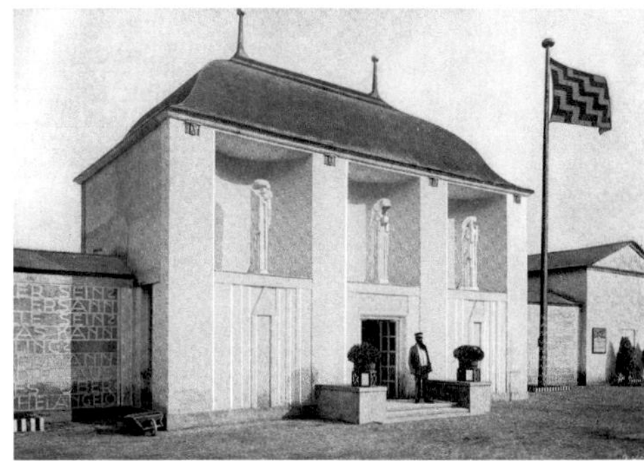

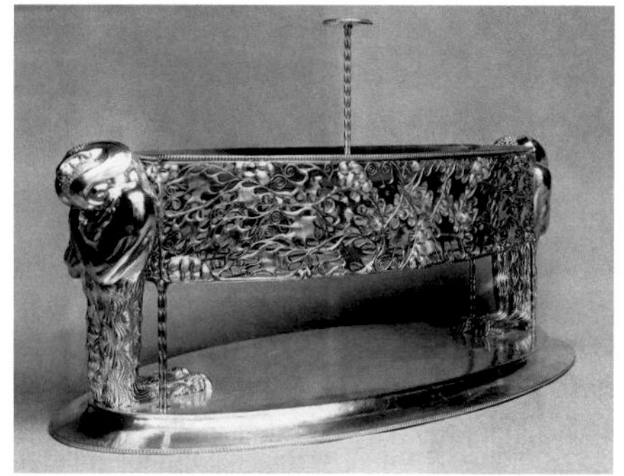

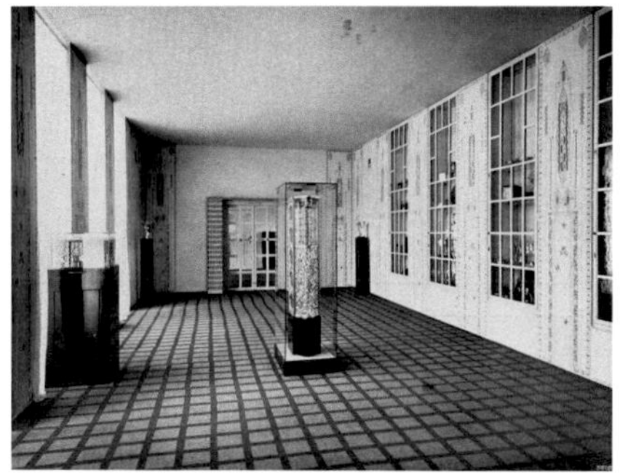

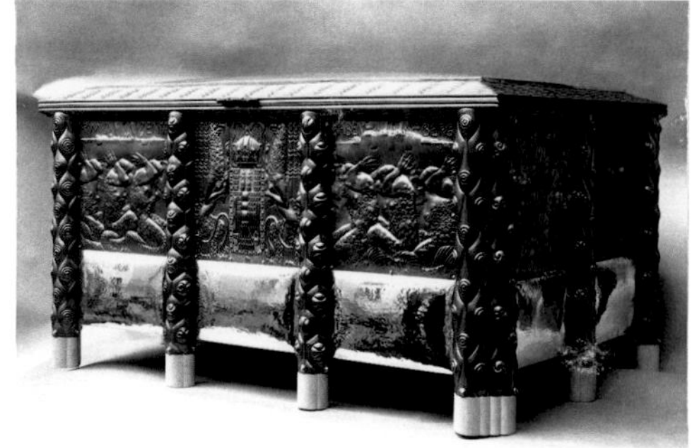

CLOCKWISE FROM TOP LEFT

FIGURE 30 Photograph of the entrance pavilion for the Kunstschau, Vienna, 1908. Designed by Josef Hoffmann. Originally published in *Der Architekt* 14 (1908).

FIGURE 31 Jardiniere, 1907. Archival photograph, MAK: Austrian Museum of Applied Arts/Contemporary Art, Vienna (WWF 94-69-3).

FIGURE 32 The *Kaiserkassette,* 1906. Archival photograph, MAK: Austrian Museum of Applied Arts/Contemporary Art, Vienna (WWF 93-31-1).

FIGURE 33 Installation photograph showing the prominence of the vitrine within gallery 50, which was dedicated to the Wiener Werkstätte, at the Kunstschau, Vienna, 1908. Originally published in *Deutsche Kunst und Dekoration,* 1908.

birds, and squirrels chased out, not sawn, to avoid rigid lines. The grapes and berries are made of different kinds of mother-of-pearl, the eyes, semi-precious stones. The treatment of every detail was punched and engraved minimally. The decoration of the flat portions are created and put together with great thought. The top of the vitrine is supported right and left by two standing female figures with raised hands, whose faces and hands are ivory. The gown falls in very stylized, flowing vertical pleats and is generously decorated, also with blue enamel; in front are long lines of mother-of-pearl. In short, it is a great accomplishment by Czeschka, whose genius now shines upon the people of Hamburg.[19]

The description of the vitrine here suggests that Czeschka began working on the piece at about the same time as the Werkstätte was completing his design for the *Kaiserkassette.* Information about the actual chronology of the design and construction is scant and this complicates the question of the intention of the Werkstätte, given its financial difficulties, in pursuing what was a hugely expensive undertaking, particularly if the vitrine had been conceived, however unlikely this may seem, for exhibition and speculative sale rather than as a commission.[20] Nonetheless, correspondence from Waerndorfer to Czeschka in the days leading up to the opening of the Kunstschau illustrates both their intention to present the vitrine to Karl Wittgenstein and the frantic pace of activity in completing it, citing work carving the ivory faces, cutting and setting the lapis lazuli stones, and fitting the glass. In a letter of May 23, Waerndorfer pronounced the vitrine finished and subsequently reported to Czeschka that he had written to Wittgenstein only the day before the opening inviting him to come and see it. As Wittgenstein was recuperating from surgery, he responded that he would be unable to visit soon; however, according to Waerndorfer, Karl's brother Paul, visiting two days after the official opening, encouraged his sibling, reporting that "the vitrine was so grand that he [Karl] had to come along" to see it.[21]

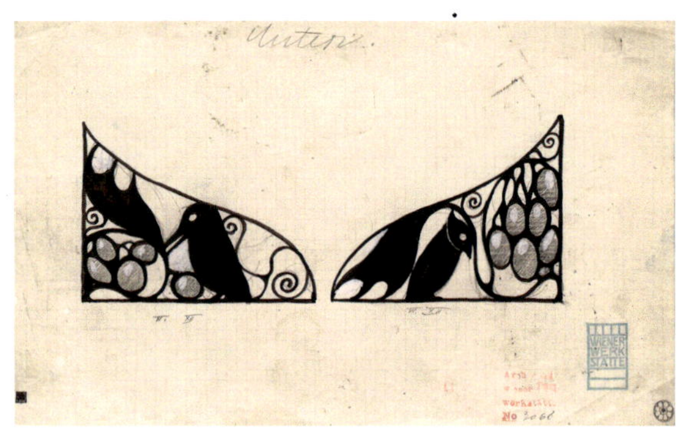

FIGURE 34 Working drawing for ornamentation on the vitrine, c. 1906–1908. Pencil, gouache, and India ink on paper. MAK: Austrian Museum of Applied Arts/Contemporary Art, Vienna (WWE 174-2).

Aside from this correspondence, surviving documentation of the project is limited to three drawings (figs. 34–36) and an entry in the Werkstätte's model book recording its order (fig. 37). The drawings, which are to scale, indicate the silhouettes of five of the pierced silver components containing the birds and fruit clusters, each of which was fashioned individually with repoussé work to raise the design of the animals and provide settings for the baroque pearls forming the clusters. One of the drawings includes pencil notations of the punched decoration of a pair of woodpeckers (the middle spotted woodpecker, *Leiopicus medius,* and the great spotted woodpecker, *Dendrocopos major*) and, curiously, a group of bulbous, egg-shaped feet that may have been considered as the base for the vitrine. The faint outline of a corresponding oval relief on the drawing of the escutcheon may have been intended as a complementary design motif; for whatever reasons, these elements were ultimately abandoned.[22] The twenty-four varieties of animals, most being native birds such as the common blackbird (*Turdus merula*) and the cuckoo (*Cuculus canorus*), include the Eurasian red squirrel, weasel, and mouse. Although each creature carries its own symbolism, as a whole they suggest a larger representation of the natural world and the vitality of nature's Tree of Life. These elements, like the otherworldly sentinel figures, play a symbolic role as guardians, partially obscuring the contents of the vitrine.

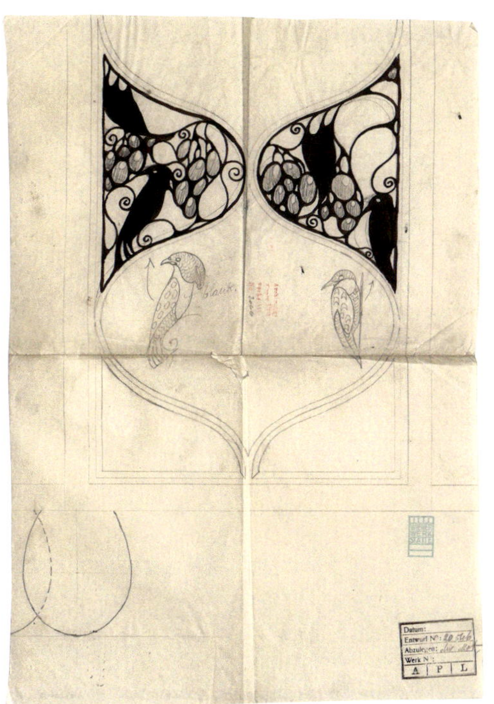

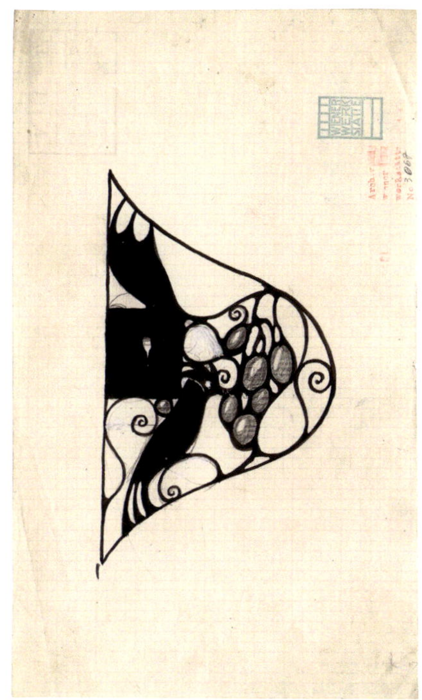

FIGURE 35 Working drawing for ornamentation on the vitrine, c. 1906–1908. Pencil, gouache, and India ink on paper. MAK: Austrian Museum of Applied Arts/Contemporary Art, Vienna (WWE 174-3).

FIGURE 36 Working drawing for ornamentation on the vitrine, c. 1906–1908. Pencil and India ink on transparent support. MAK: Austrian Museum of Applied Arts/Contemporary Art, Vienna (WWE 174-1).

FIGURE 37 Entry for the vitrine in the Wiener Werkstätte model book, c. 1908. MAK: Austrian Museum of Applied Arts/Contemporary Art, Vienna (WWMB 9-S-1000).

1000

VITRINE

SILBER, GETRIEBENE HANDARBEIT, M. PERLSCHALEN
V. HALBEDELSTEINEN BESETZT, EMAILIERTEN FIGUREN
SPIEGELGLASFÜLLUNGEN, DECKPLATTE AUS ONIX, V. HOLZSOCKEL A. MARKASSAR
SILBER 925-1000. 34.318 g à 12 HEL. 4118.16
ABG. 154.35 PUNZ 216.20 VERS. 114.90 STEINE 899.70
GLÄSER 55— GLASSCHL. 73— MARMOR 56.26 ELFENB. 21.40
SCHRAUBEN 38— DRAHTZIEHER 30— TISCHLERMAT. 25—
EMAILEUR 186.10 PERLMUTTERGRAVEUR 145—
SCHLOSS 10— POL. 36.60 GLASBIEGER 45—
HOLZMODELKASTEN 25— DREHERH— | 6249.67
LOHN. HOSSFELD 1412.87 1228.44 ERBRICH. 2226.82 1825.32
MAYER 235.65 152.75 WABAK 1383.63 871.29
BERGER 91.63 56.42 ALBRECHT 228.75 171—
PLASINSKY 395.52 205.40 CERHAN 62.63 39.06
WEBER 791/2. 65 51.68 | 4601.36
K 25 000.— | 10851.03

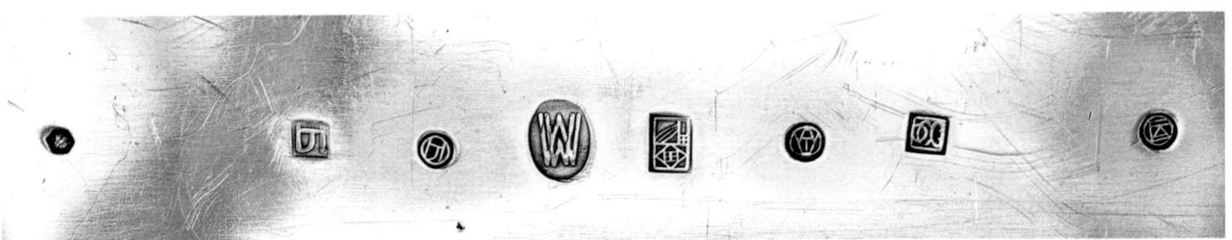

FIGURE 38 Punch marks on interior base of vitrine, left to right:
1. Head of Diana (hexagonal; indicating the purity of the silver — assayed here as sterling grade; the letter A, indicating that the vitrine was made in Vienna)
2. Josef Hoffmann, Artistic Director
3. Josef Holi, Metalworker (marking error for Josef Hoszfeld, silversmith)
4. Wiener Werkstätte mark
5. Wiener Werkstätte mark
6. Alois Wabak, Silversmith
7. Carl Otto Czeschka, Designer
8. Adolf Erbrich, Silversmith

The model book ledger entry serves, alongside the host of marks punched into the silver (fig. 38), as documentation of the immense amount of time, material, and varied expertise required to produce the vitrine — the most complex and expensive single object the Werkstätte ever made. A detailed list of materials and their corresponding costs indicates the expense: the sterling-grade silver is valued at 4,118 kronen (crowns); the assorted semiprecious stones, at nearly 900 kronen, and a host of tasks — from glass-shaping to polishing and enameling — at 6,253 kronen. To this figure, another 4,601 kronen were assigned to the pay of several Werkstätte craftsmen, among them "Hossfeld" (*sic;* Josef Hoszfeld, 1869–1918), Adolph Erbrich (1874–?), Alfred Mayer (1873–?), Josef Berger (1874 or 1875–?), Alois Wabak (active 1905–1929), and Josef Weber (dates unknown), and three named, but otherwise — so far — unidentified craftsmen: Albrecht, Cerhan, and Plasinsky. Only Erbrich was publicly identified as a craftsman at the time of the exhibition; given that his expense was far more than that incurred for any of the others and nearly half of the total paid to the participants, it is not entirely unexpected that he be named, but it was still unusual for the Werkstätte.[23] Almost every design journal covering the Kunstschau cited Czeschka as the designer. However, the original inclusion of Hoffmann's mark on the silver base of the vitrine and a discrepancy within the model book entry have provoked questions about his possible role as a co-designer of the overall form or concept for the vitrine.[24] The model book entry includes a stamped ink cipher for Hoffmann that is struck through with pencil marks and replaced below with Czeschka's mark, also rendered in pencil, rather than stamped. While the reason for the appearance of Hoffmann's mark is unknown, as are the particulars of the correction of the entry, such corrections are not unprecedented in the ledgers and appear for other works, not only Czeschka's, originally stamped with Hoffmann's mark. In any regard, even as Hoffmann served (previously, along with Moser) as the artistic director of the Werkstätte, there appears to be no question about the public attribution of the vitrine for visitors to the Kunstschau: the base of the protective

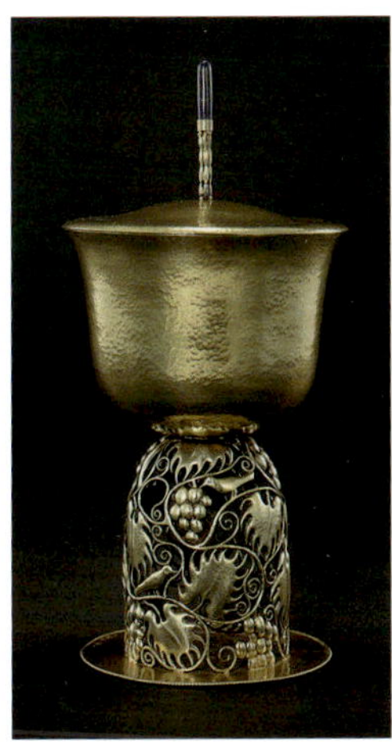

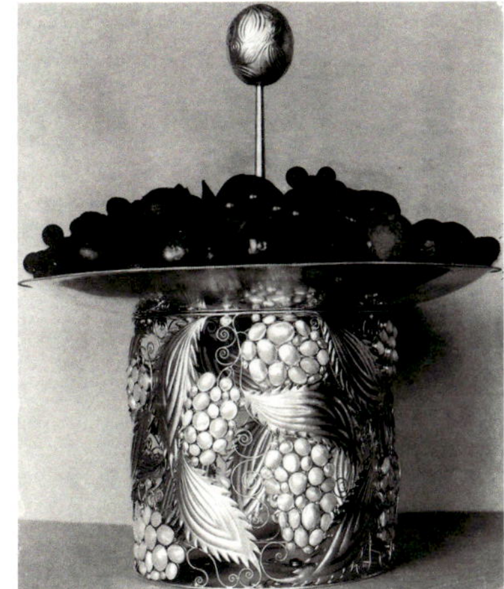

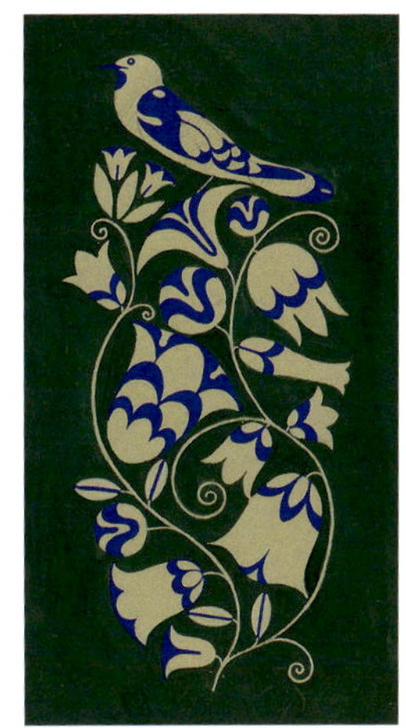

FIGURE 39 Loving cup with cover, c. 1909. Silver gilt and lapis lazuli. Detroit Institute of Arts, Gift of George G. Booth (23.161).

FIGURE 40 Centerpiece, with leaf and grape motif, c. 1908–14. Archival photograph, MAK: Austrian Museum of Applied Arts/Contemporary Art, Vienna (WWF 95-176-4).

FIGURE 41 Design for an embroidery, c. 1911. Gouache on paper. Museum für Kunst und Gewerbe, Hamburg, 1976 (E. 1976.312).

FIGURE 42 Necklace, 1910. Gold and opals. MAK: Austrian Museum of Applied Arts/Contemporary Art, Vienna, purchased from the Wiener Werkstätte (WI 1061).

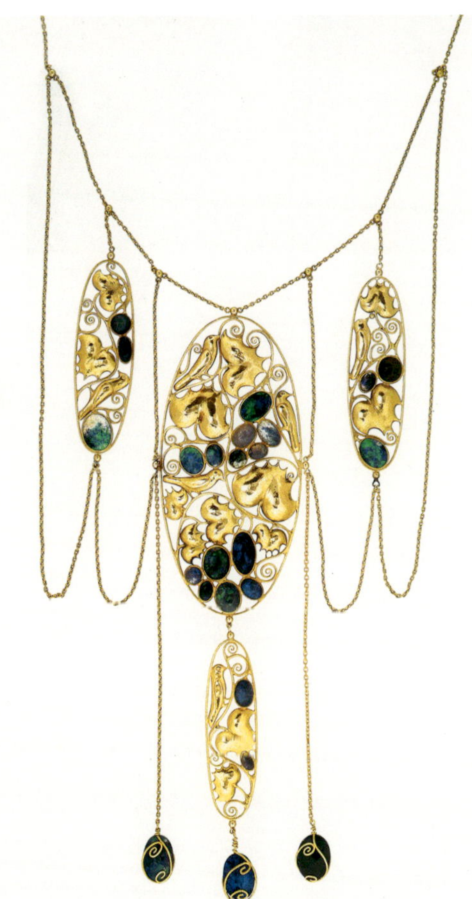

case in which it was exhibited carried the identifying plaque: "Prof. C. O. Czeschka."[25]

He was, however, no longer a resident of Vienna by the time the vitrine arrived at the Kunstschau, having left for a new teaching position at the School of Applied Arts in Hamburg in October of 1907 and

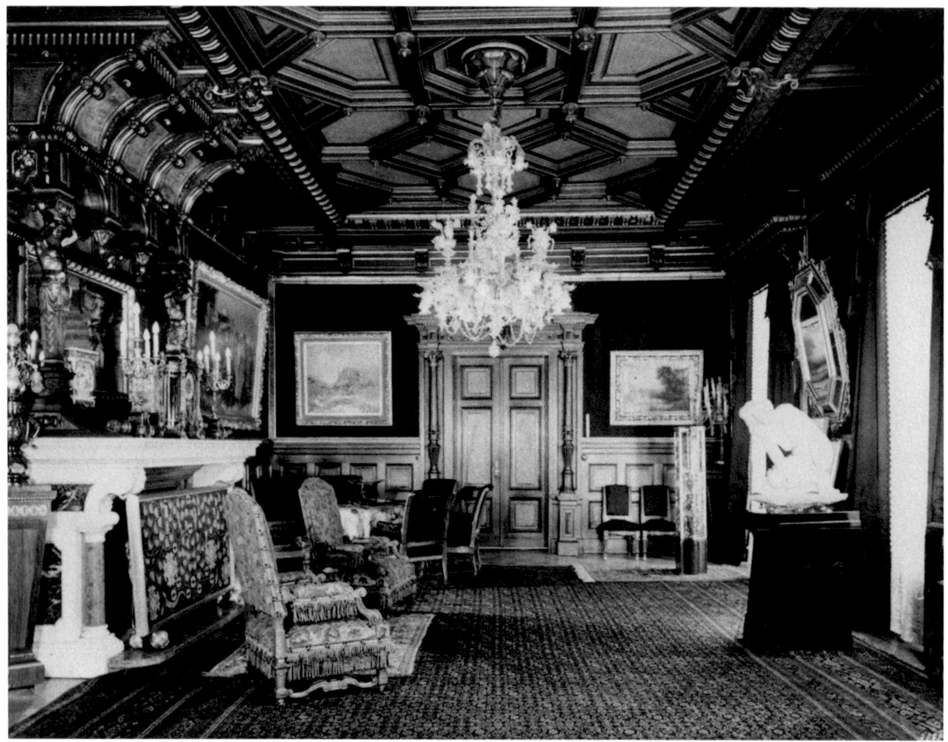

FIGURE 43 The vitrine (far right) and the fire screen (far left) on display in the Red Salon in the Palais Wittgenstein, Vienna, c. 1910. Photograph reproduced from Tobias Natter, *Die Welt von Klimt, Schiele und Kokoschka: Sammler und Mäzene* (Cologne: DuMont, 2003), p. 46; Österreichische Nationalbibliothek, Vienna.

having formally become a citizen of that city in June of 1908. Czeschka's move was lamented in the Austrian press as "another disaster . . . which has recently befallen us in silence. In brief, we lose C. O. Czeschka. He's won a professorship at the Hamburg Art School." The reporter added that his departure was the result of neglect by Vienna's School of Applied Arts, which failed to award him a full professorship.[26] He continued to submit a quantity of designs for the Werkstätte through 1914, including textiles, two versions of a silver-gilt cup (fig. 39), a centerpiece (fig. 40), a design for embroidery (fig. 41), and a necklace (fig. 42), all of which directly recall the bird, leaf, and fruit cluster motif of the vitrine.

Karl Wittgenstein's purchase of the vitrine was reported by several reviewers of the Kunstschau, who spoke of the object as "the most important work of decorative art" in modern Vienna.[27] Whether or not Wittgenstein had commissioned or otherwise prompted the work remains unclear, as Waerndorfer's letter to Czeschka of June 5, 1908, written shortly after the Kunstschau opened, confirms only Wittgenstein's purchase of the vitrine in that prior week for thirty thousand crowns. The praise and lament that Waerndorfer then offers point directly to the Werkstätte's precarious financial state and its dependence upon such clients: "You cannot imagine how grand it turned out. I weep tears of blood that the vitrine does not belong to me, it's a piece that will never be made again, and if we did not need the money so urgently he would never have acquired it."[28]

The vitrine was accorded a place of honor within the Palais Wittgenstein's Red Salon (fig. 43), which was far from a *Gesamtkunstwerk* in the manner of the rooms at Hochreith. The few pieces of progressive art within the space — Klimt paintings, the fire screen by Czeschka and Hoffmann, and a sculpture of Beethoven by Max Klinger, along with the vitrine — provided the heavy, nineteenth-century interior with a new form of opulence for the modern century.

Adolph Loos, the Viennese architect and design critic, decried much of what the Kunstschau represented, including the vitrine and its ornamentation, as antithetical to modernist ideology. Part of his attack, written in 1908, approached the subject by invoking the gingerbread designed by Czeschka and Moser and sold by the spouses of the Werkstätte members to visitors to the exhibition:

> *I do not accept the objection that ornament is a source of increased pleasure in life for cultured people, the objection expressed in the exclamation, "But, if the ornament is beautiful!" For me, and with me, for all people of culture, ornament is not a source of increased pleasure in life. When I want to eat a piece of gingerbread, I choose a piece that is plain, not a piece shaped like a heart, or a baby, or a cavalryman, covered over and over in decoration. A fifteenth-century man would not have understood me, but all modern people will.*[29]

Loos's proclamations of austerity and authentic expression may have shaped the seeds of a new modernism, but such developments neither ended the Werkstätte's approach to ornamentation and craft in the ensuing years, nor diminished the importance of its work as an alternate path to that of the Bauhaus School's machine-age functionalism of the 1920s and, through the lens of postmodernism, as an aesthetic of emotion rather than rationalism. Even so, within a decade, World War I and the dissolution of the Austro-Hungarian empire would erase virtually all the traces of the circumstances that fostered the creation of the vitrine — the great wealth and patronage of Karl Wittgenstein and the creative energy of Czeschka and the Wiener Werkstätte to fashion nearly two hundred pounds of silver, gemstones, and glass into a lavish testimonial to Vienna's moment as the leading international center of progressive art.

The vitrine's function as a physical container seems superfluous. Instead, like some secular reliquary of exquisite richness, it holds the aspirations of the Werkstätte, the dreams of a Wittgenstein, and the virtuosity of its designer and those craftspeople who fashioned it. It stands less as a vitrine made simply to display its contents clearly through the glass than as an elemental silver forest to obscure and mystify; less as a stage for the theater of Viennese design in the first decade of the twentieth century than as a leading actor in the play itself.

NOTES

In developing this essay, I was assisted by a number of exceptional colleagues to whom I am deeply grateful. I am especially indebted to Christian Witt-Dörring, curator at MAK: the Austrian Museum of Applied Arts/Contemporary Arts, Vienna; Elisabeth Schmuttermeier, Curator, Metal Collection and Wiener Werkstätte Archive, MAK, Vienna; Maria Luise-Jesch, Project Staff, Wiener Werkstätte Archive, MAK, Vienna; Hella Häussler, independent scholar, Hamburg; and Senta Siller, independent scholar, Nauen, Germany. Special thanks go to Alessandra Comini, University Distinguished Professor of Art History Emerita at Southern Methodist University, Dallas, for her limitless enthusiasm for and knowledge of early twentieth-century Viennese art and for being a source of inspiration for my own efforts in this realm. My gratitude is extended to Margaret and Pierre Stonborough and the other descendants of Karl Wittgenstein for their insights and to my colleagues at the DMA, Fran Baas, Associate Conservator, and Samantha Robinson, formerly a McDermott Curatorial Intern for Decorative Arts and Design and now the Museum's Digital Collections Content Coordinator for Decorative Arts and Design, for their tireless efforts in helping me realize the exhibition *Modern Opulence in Vienna: The Wittgenstein Vitrine,* the research for which provided the foundation of this text. Any errors within this essay are entirely my own.

1 The decoration and materials of the vitrine made it undeniably lavish at the time and especially in comparison with the ornamental restraint of earlier designs by Hoffmann and Moser or relative to the early modernist philosophy of the designer and Werkstätte critic Adolph Loos; see Kirk Varnedoe, *Vienna 1900: Art, Architecture, and Design* (New York: Museum of Modern Art, 1986), for more recent criticism of the vitrine as an exemplar of the shift in the Werkstätte aesthetic by 1908.

2 Period journals and the documentation of the Wiener Werkstätte archives held by the MAK (the Austrian Museum of Applied Arts), Vienna, including surviving photographs, drawings, and model book entries, suggest that the quantity of Czeschka's contributions to the Werkstätte is significantly more extensive than identified, extant objects might suggest. Although fragmentary, the Werkstätte archives at the MAK serve as a crucial source for research on any designs by the organization, including that of the vitrine. There are numerous publications on the topic of the Wiener Werkstätte; a fuller accounting here is beyond the scope of this essay, but of particular interest to the reader will be Michael Huey, ed., *Viennese Silver: Modern Design, 1780–1918* (Ostfildern-Ruit, Germany: Hatje Cantz, 2003) for a fuller appreciation of the Werkstätte's design antecedents as well as biographical studies of the metalworkers there. Aspects of Czeschka's career are detailed in relatively few publications, but are to be found in Heinz Spielmann and Hella Häussler, *Carl Otto Czeschka, 1878–1960: Ein Wiener Künstler und die Hamburger Wirtschaft* (Hamburg: Handelskammer with the Elsbeth Weichmann Gesellschaft, 2011); Heinz Spielmann, *Carl Otto Czeschka: Aspekte seines Lebenswerkes* (Hamburg: Interversa, 1978); and Giovanni Fanelli, *Carl Otto Czeschka dalla Secessione Viennese all'Art Déco* (Florence: Cantini, 1990).

3 Spielmann and Häussler 2011, p. 21.

4 *Jugendstil* (German for "youth style") is the German and Austrian version of Art Nouveau. See Spielmann 1978, which includes an untitled chronology of the artist, and Spielmann and Häussler 2011, p. 66. Unless otherwise noted, all working dates and biographical details are referenced from Senta Siller, "Carl Otto Czeschka, 1878–1960: Leben und Werk" (PhD diss., Technical University of Berlin, 1992), the most comprehensive study of Czeschka's career to date. Additional details of Czeschka's career before 1908 are framed by extant works and disparate archival and secondary sources, including material in the archives of the Wiener Werkstätte at the MAK, Vienna.

5 Czeschka was formally accepted as a full member of the Secession in November of 1900; he exhibited with the group in 1900, 1902, and 1904.

6 Christian Witt-Dörring, et al., *Koloman Moser: Designing Modern Vienna, 1897–1907* (New York: Prestel Verlag, 2013), p. 80.

7 Originally published in *Hohe Warte* 1 (Leipzig and Vienna: R. Voigtländers Verlag, 1904–1905); as translated in Jan Ernst Adlmann, *Vienna Moderne, 1898–1918: An Early Encounter between Taste and Utility*, exh. cat. Sarah Campbell Blaffer Gallery, University of Houston (Houston: The Gallery, 1978), pp. 87–88.

8 Christian Witt-Dörring, "Individuality in Viennese Modern Design around 1900: Pro and Con," in *Birth of the Modern: Style and Identity in Vienna, 1900* (Munich: Hirmer Verlag, 2011), p. 79.

9 Julius Baum, "Wiener Werkstätte Neustiftgasse 32," *Deutsche Kunst und Dekoration* 19 (1906–1907), 443–56. See also Werner J. Schweiger, *Wiener Werkstaette: Design in Vienna, 1903–1932*, transl. Alexander Lieven (New York: Abbeville Press, 1984), pp. 163–67.

10 First published in 1906–1907; see Baum 1906–1907; see also "Welche Mittel hat der für das Kunstgewerbe entwerfende Künstler, . . ." *Deutsche Kunst und Dekoration* 19 (1906–1907), illus. p. 466.

11 See Heinz Spielmann, *Die Jugendstil—Sammlung 1: Künstler A–F* (Hamburg: Museum für Kunst und Gewerbe, 1979), pp. 219–20. One sketch, from 1898, includes a pencil notation identifying the armor as that of "Maximilian I" and a location of the "Hofmuseum." The Neue Burg at Vienna's Hofburg Palace now exhibits the imperial arms and armor collections of the Kunsthistorisches Museum, including the subject of these sketches.

12 Siller 1992, p. 21.

13 Colin B. Bailey and John Bruce Collins, *Gustav Klimt: Modernism in the Making*, exh. cat., National Gallery of Canada, Ottawa (New York: Abrams, 2001), p. 101.

14 Ashbee's work would have been well known to Czeschka by 1906. Both Ashbee and Charles Rennie Mackintosh (whom Czeschka also could have met during his visit to London, as Klimt did) had participated in Secession exhibitions, the former having exhibited with the group in 1902, 1905, and 1906 as an honorary member and the latter (along with Margaret and Francis MacDonald and Herbert MacNair) notably contributing a furnished room to the exhibition of 1900. The Glasgow School's predilection for attenuated figures and Ashbee's own decorations drawn from nature provided a certain resonance with the interests of European artists and designers, including Czeschka and many of his Viennese colleagues; see Alan Crawford, *C. R. Ashbee: Architect, Designer and Romantic Socialist* (New Haven: Yale University Press, 1985), pp. 410–14.

15 Siller 1992, p. 110.

16 The current disposition of these presumptive study versions is unknown. There is no known precedent for sculptural figures or caryatids in other Werkstätte *furniture* from this period, but, in 1934, following the dissolution of the organization, Hoffmann would design a unique wood and glass vitrine with four classicized caryatids supporting the upper case (MAK Collection, Vienna). Even so, in architectural decoration and small ceramics (including the putti designs by Michael Powolny that were exhibited on pedestals near the vitrine at the Kunstschau in 1908), sculptural figures played a commanding role in the output of the Werkstätte.

17 The massive jardiniere (location currently unknown) with the twin satyr-like figures suggests a mythological and classical counterpoint to the vitrine with its angelic knights—the sacred and the profane. The casket is decorated with ten repoussé panels, the central front panel featuring the coat of arms of Imperial Austria flanked by two panels of mermen with ships; see Schweiger 1984, p. 55, and "Kassette für den Kaiser von Oesterreich," *Deutsche Kunst und Dekoration* 19 (1906–1907), pp. 416–20. The casket is currently in the collection of the Österreichische Nationalbibliothek (Austrian National Library), Vienna. By chance, the timing of the emperor's visit coincided with the start of Czeschka's formal relationship with the Werkstätte, making the casket one of the very first silver designs he produced for the atelier. For a detailed accounting of the Kunstschau, with inventories and insightful commentary upon the works exhibited in gallery 50, including the casket and vitrine, see Elisabeth Schmuttermeier, "Die Wiener Werkstätte auf der Kunstschau 1908," in *Gustav Klimt und die Kunstschau 1908*, ed. Agnes Husslein-Arco and Alfred Weidinger (Munich: Prestel Verlag, 2008), pp. 434–41.

18 Fritz Waerndorfer to Carl Otto Czeschka, May 23, 1908. My thanks to Claudia Banz, Head of Collections Art and Design—Biedermeier to Present, Museum für Kunst und Gewerbe, Hamburg, for providing copies of unpublished letters (in the collection of the Hamburg Museum für Kunst und Gewerbe), dated May 19, May 23, and June 5, 1908, from Fritz Waerndorfer to Czeschka

19 Ludwig Hevesi, "Kunstschau 1908" (May 31, 1908), in *Altkunst-Neukunst: Wien, 1894–1908*, ed. Otto Breicha (1909; repr., Klagenfurt, Austria: Ritter Verlag, 1986), pp. 315–16. See also Schmuttermeier 2008, p. 436. The "grapes" of the vitrine are of cut baroque pearls. The identification of the gender of the twin figures as female in this text may suggest an allusion to other female warrior figures popularized at the time, including the valkyries of Norse mythology as featured in Richard Wagner's opera, *Der Ring des Nibelungen*—a subject with which Czeschka was well acquainted.

20 See Siller's review of references to the vitrine in unpublished letters, dated May 19, May 23, and June 5, 1908, from Fritz Waerndorfer to Czeschka, indicating the sale of the vitrine to Karl Wittgenstein for thirty thousand crowns after the Kunstschau opened to the public in June; Siller 1992, pp. 109–11.

21 Fritz Waerndorfer to Carl Otto Czeschka, June 5, 1908.

22 The ebony-veneered base (or socle) upon which the silver case rests has undergone restoration (see the essay by Fran Baas, the associate conservator for objects at the Dallas Museum of Art, in this volume). During the restoration of the base, the original upper molding of ebony was revealed, as was the original substrate, albeit trimmed from its original height. The underside of the silver cabinet has a silver flange that follows the contours of the hollow socle; the flange is pierced and countersunk at regular intervals to allow screws to be placed through it, securing the cabinet to the inner side of the substrate. Two large bosses, each threaded and located at either side of the underside of the silver case, serve no apparent function. Whether these were originally intended as additional attachment points for the socle as presently designed—which is unlikely or ill-considered, given their location and near inaccessibility—or for a base of a different design proposed at some point during the original construction is unknown. As to the alternate egg-shaped feet suggested by one surviving drawing, it is interesting to note the precedent of other bulbous foot shapes used by Hoffmann and Moser, notably the carved and gilded wooden spherical feet on the Wittgenstein fire screen co-designed by Hoffmann and Czeschka. The subtle wit of using egg-shaped feet for a vitrine covered with bird designs is appealing, although the lowered overall height of the vitrine would have rendered it proportionally awkward and greatly diminished the visual impact of the caryatid figures.

23 See Hevesi, "Kunstschau 1908," p. 315; and "the hall of the Wiener Werkstätte with a silver case Czeschka designed and Erbrich executed" in "Ausstellungen," *Die Werkkunst* 3 (October 1907–September 1908), p. 319.

24 Sotheby's, New York, *Important Vienna Secessionist Works of Art,* November 19, 1983, lot 500 (auction catalogue).

25 The plaques can be seen in uncropped photographs of the vitrine held in the MAK Wiener Werkstätte archives. The photographs have been published with the plaques cropped out; see Emil Utitz, "Münchens Ernte 1908," *Deutsche Kunst und Dekoration* 23 (1908–1909), pp. 164–74.

26 Ludwig Hevesi, "C. O. Czeschka" (August 9, 1907), in Breicha, ed., 1909/1986, pp. 236–40. For dates of Czeschka's move to Hamburg, see Siller 1992.

27 Ludwig Hevesi, "Kunstschau Wien 1908," *Zeitschrift für bildende Kunst* 19, no. 43 (1908), p. 247. A later publication referencing the Kunstschau describes "a magnificent silver cabinet, which was bought for over 50,000 [*sic*] kronen on the opening day by Herr von Wittgenstein, one of Austria's chief patrons of modern art" (Levetus, "'Wiener Werkstätte', Vienna," 1911, 196). Even at the actual price of thirty thousand crowns, the cost was extraordinary and well beyond that of any other single silver object that the Vienna Werkstätte produced. My thanks to the scholar Christian Witt-Dörring for his comments about the possibility that the vitrine could have, indeed, been made for exhibition purposes; his suggestion reinforces the assessment of the Werkstätte's poor financial management and its overly ambitious commitments at the time of Moser's departure from the group and of the conception and production of the work; e-mail message to the author, November 8, 2014.

28 Fritz Waerndorfer to Carl Otto Czeschka, June 5, 1908.

29 Adolph Loos, *Ornament and Crime: Selected Essays,* ed. Adolf Opel (Riverside, Calif.: Ariadne Press, 1998), p. 169.

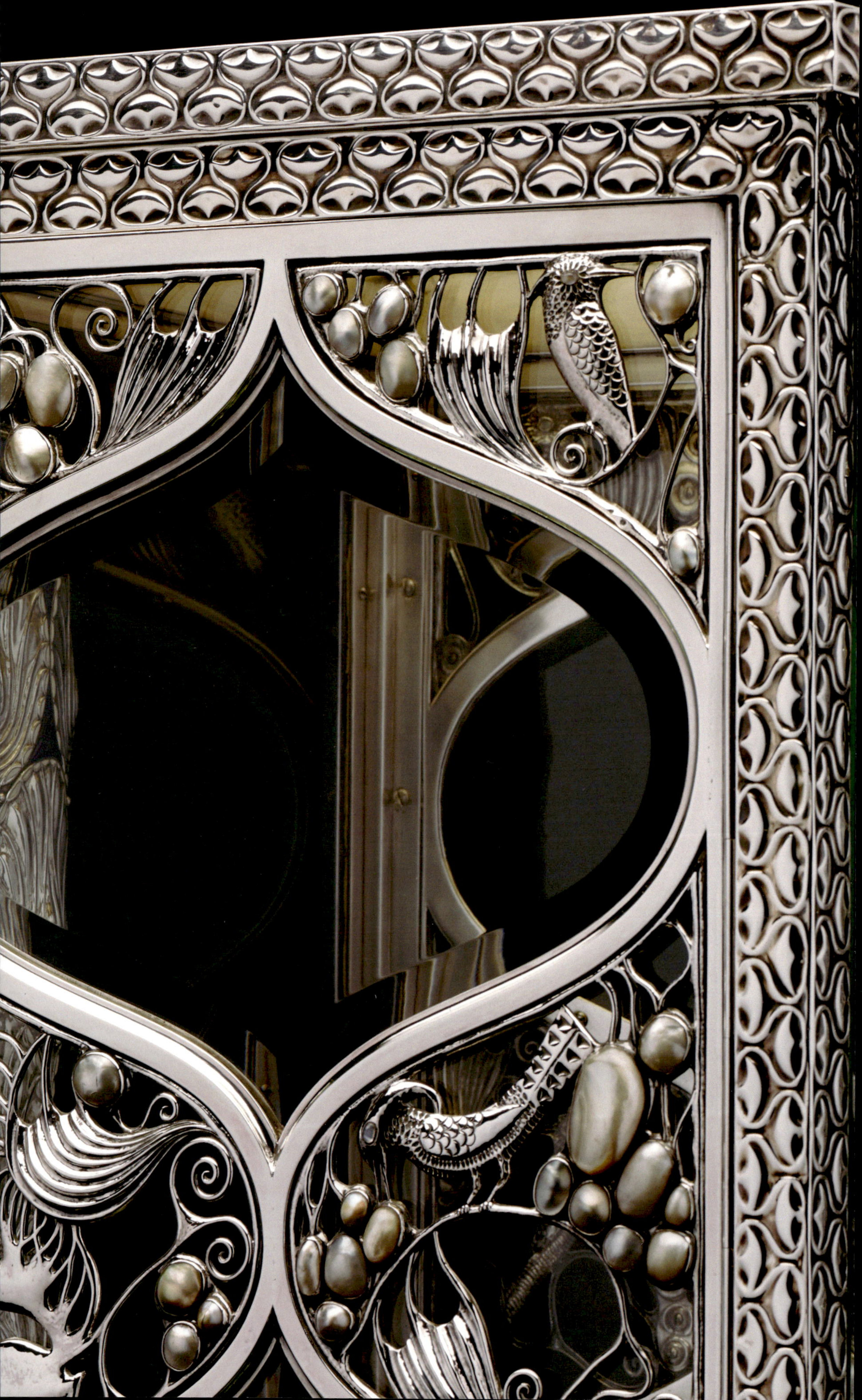

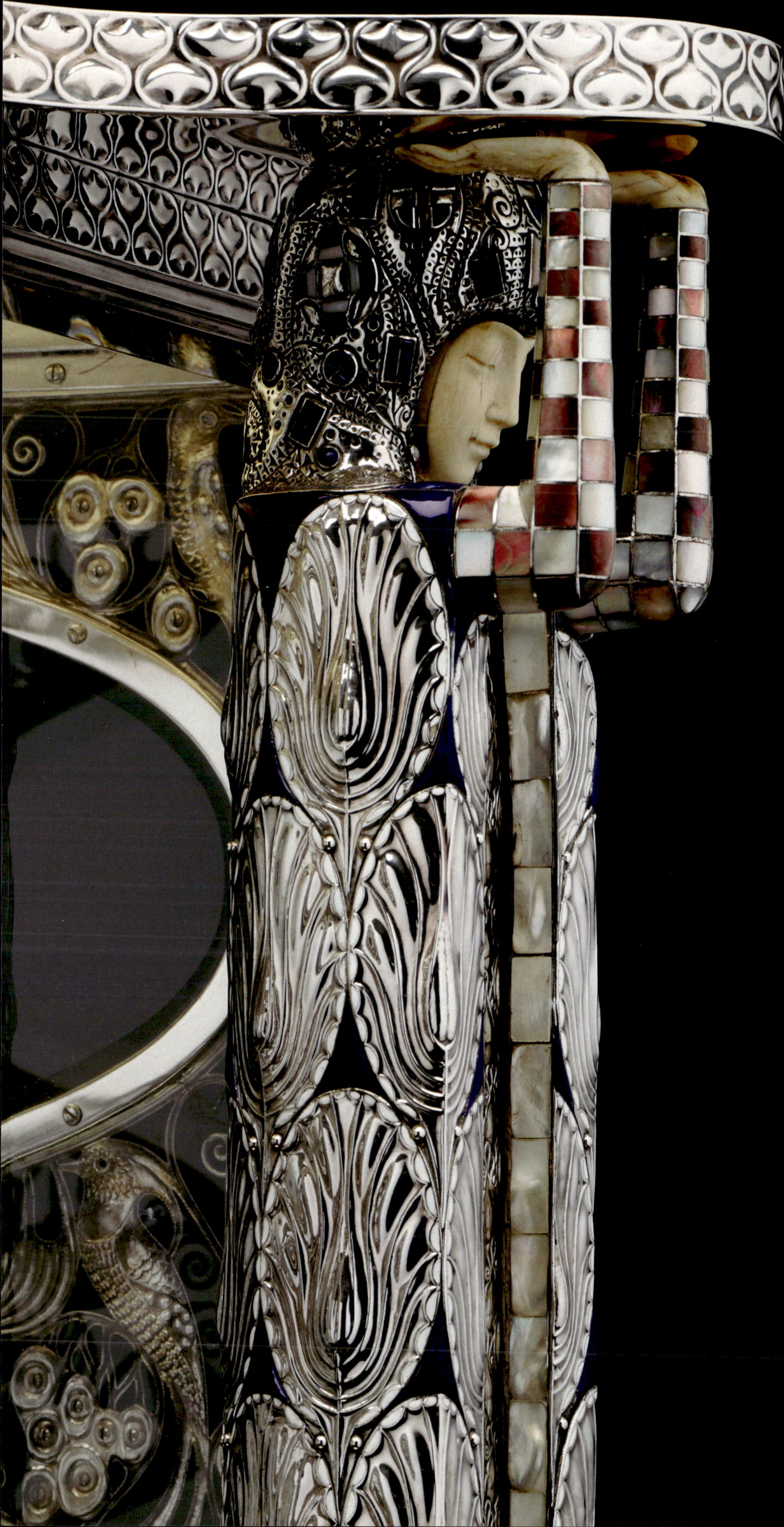

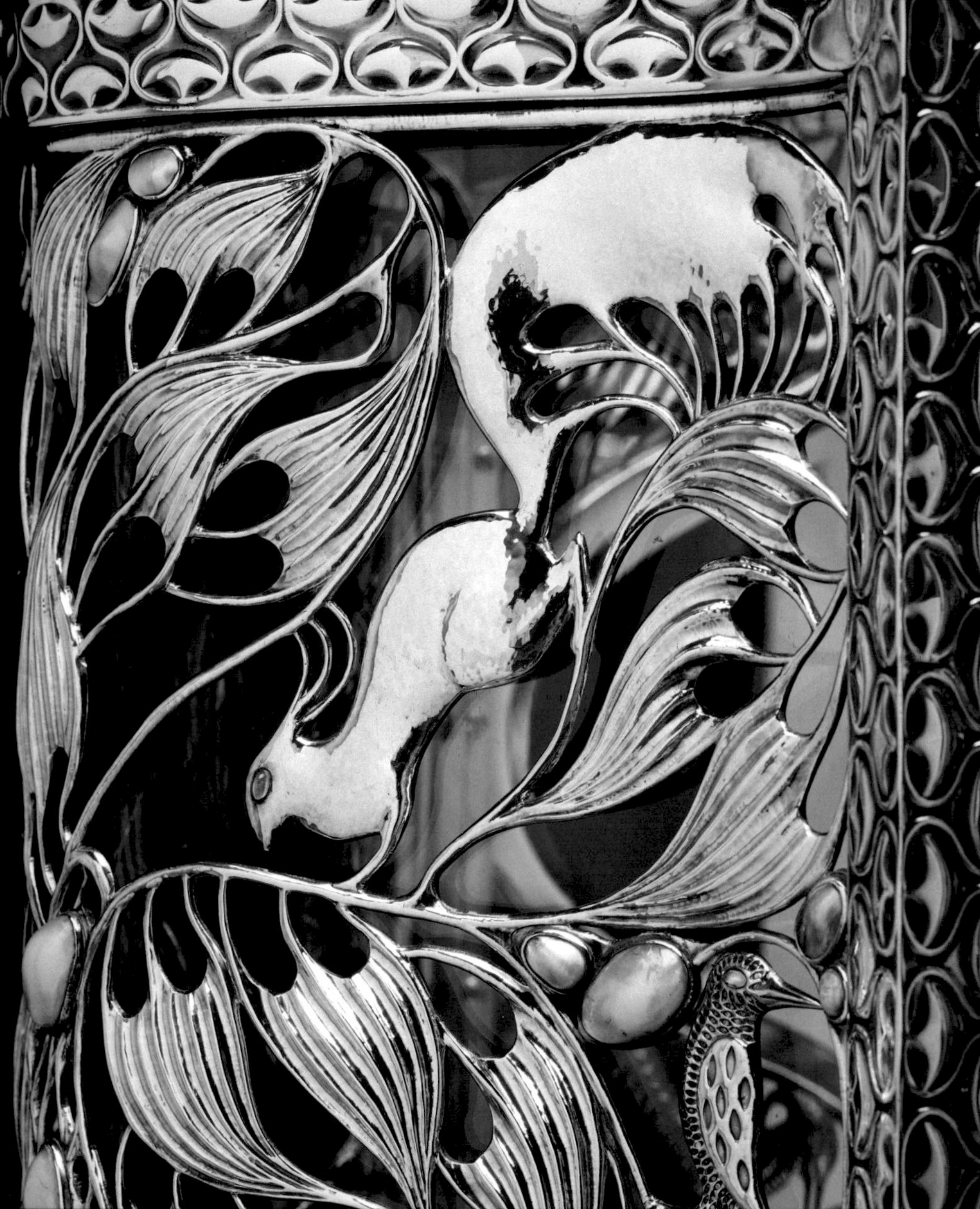

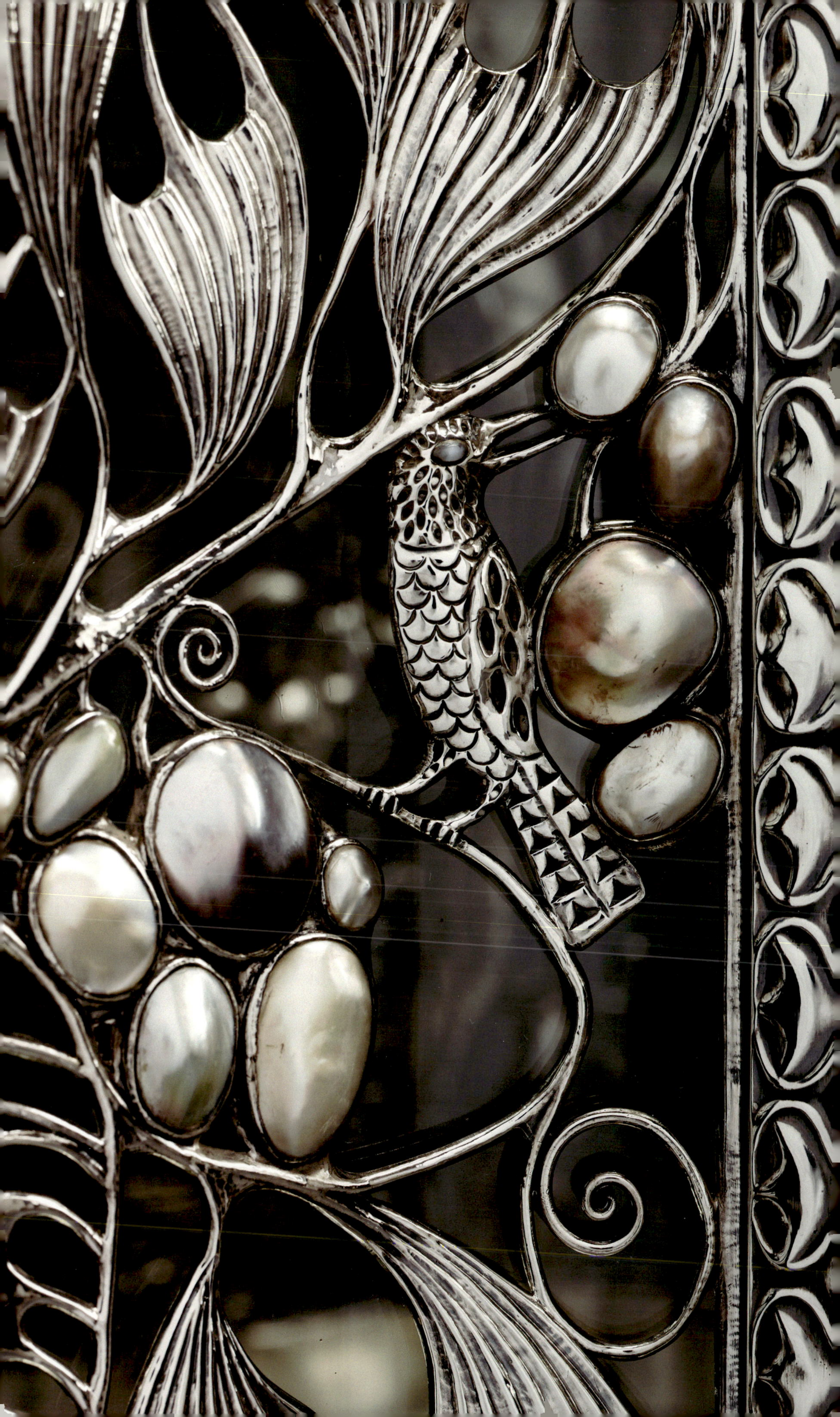

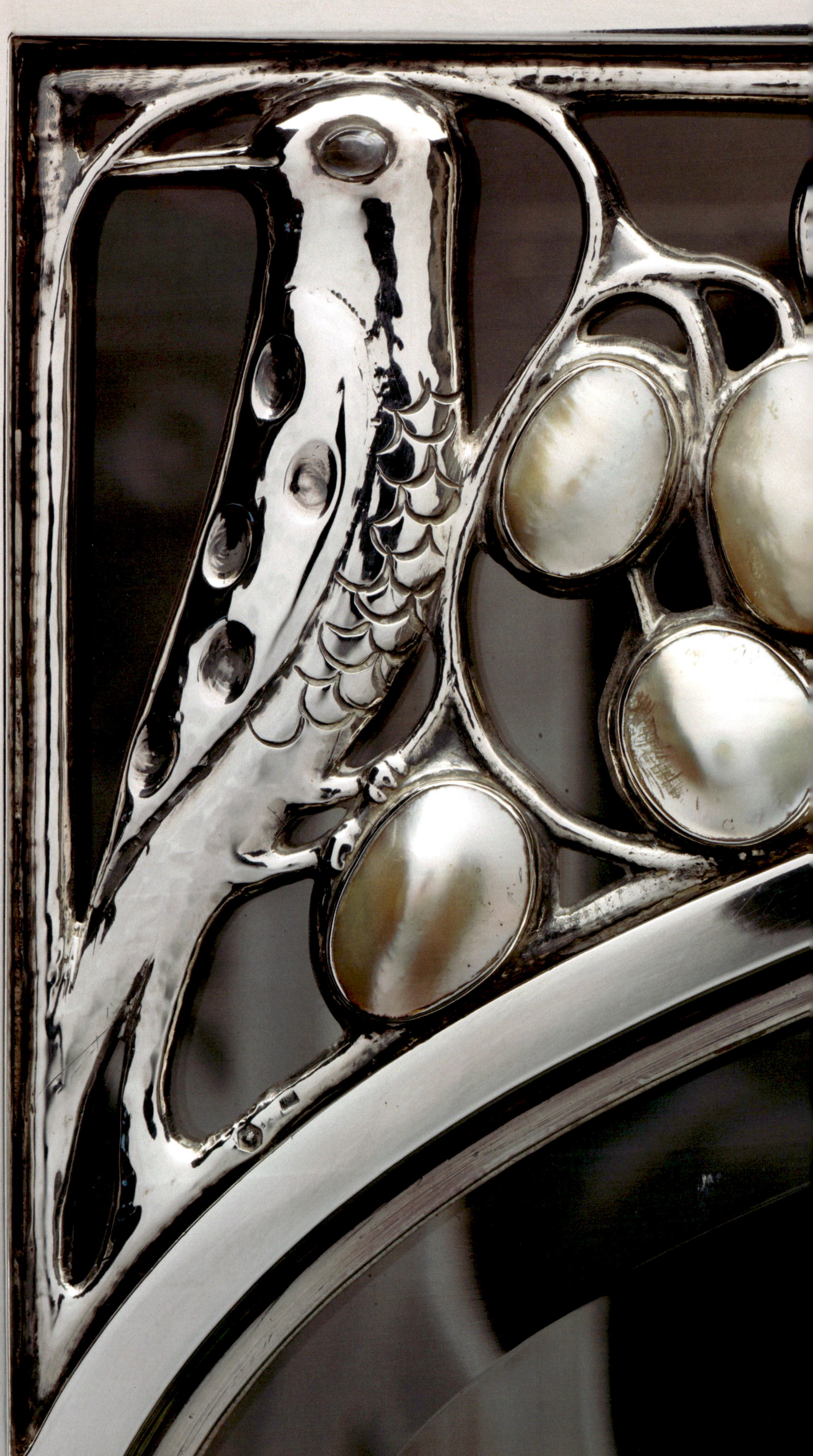

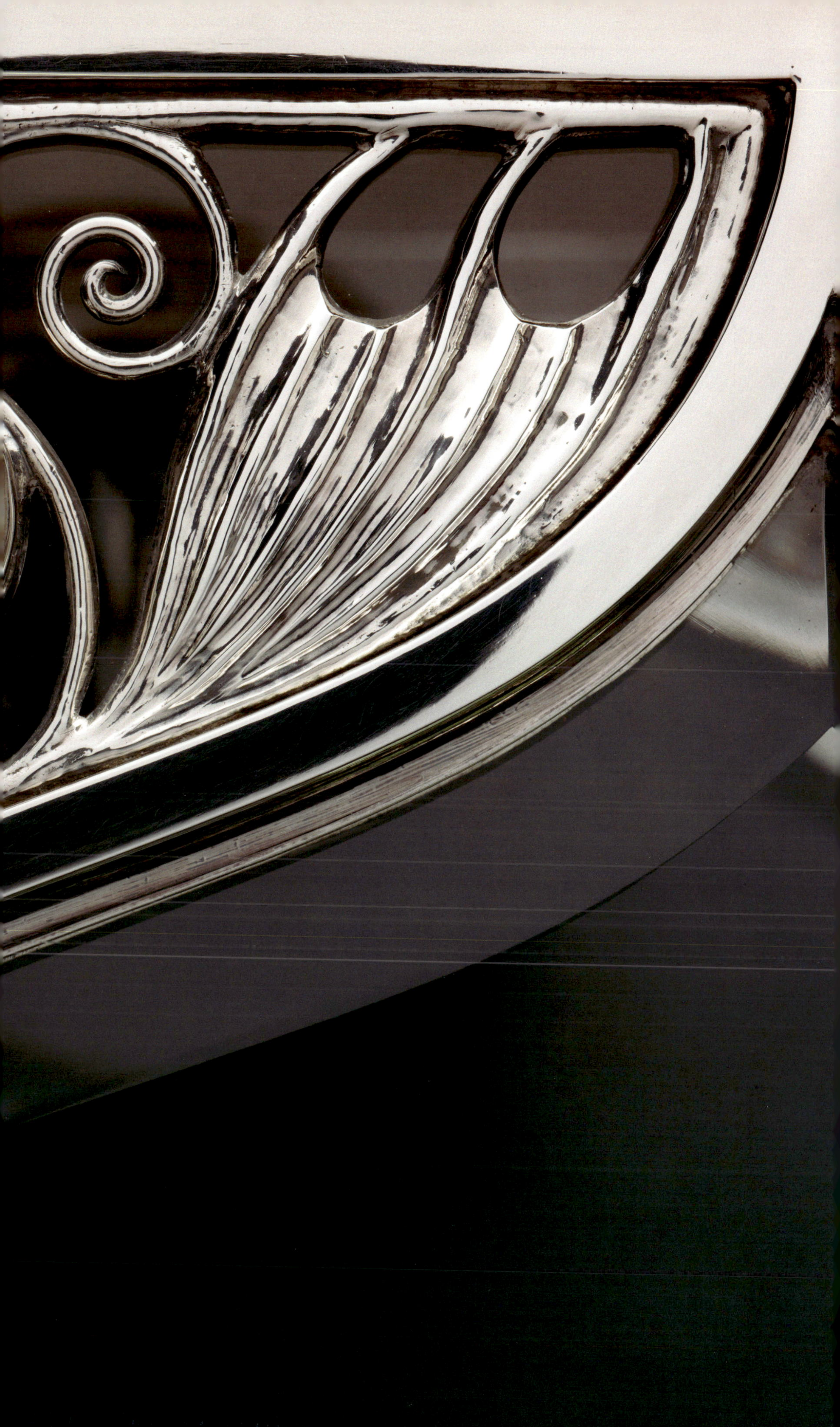

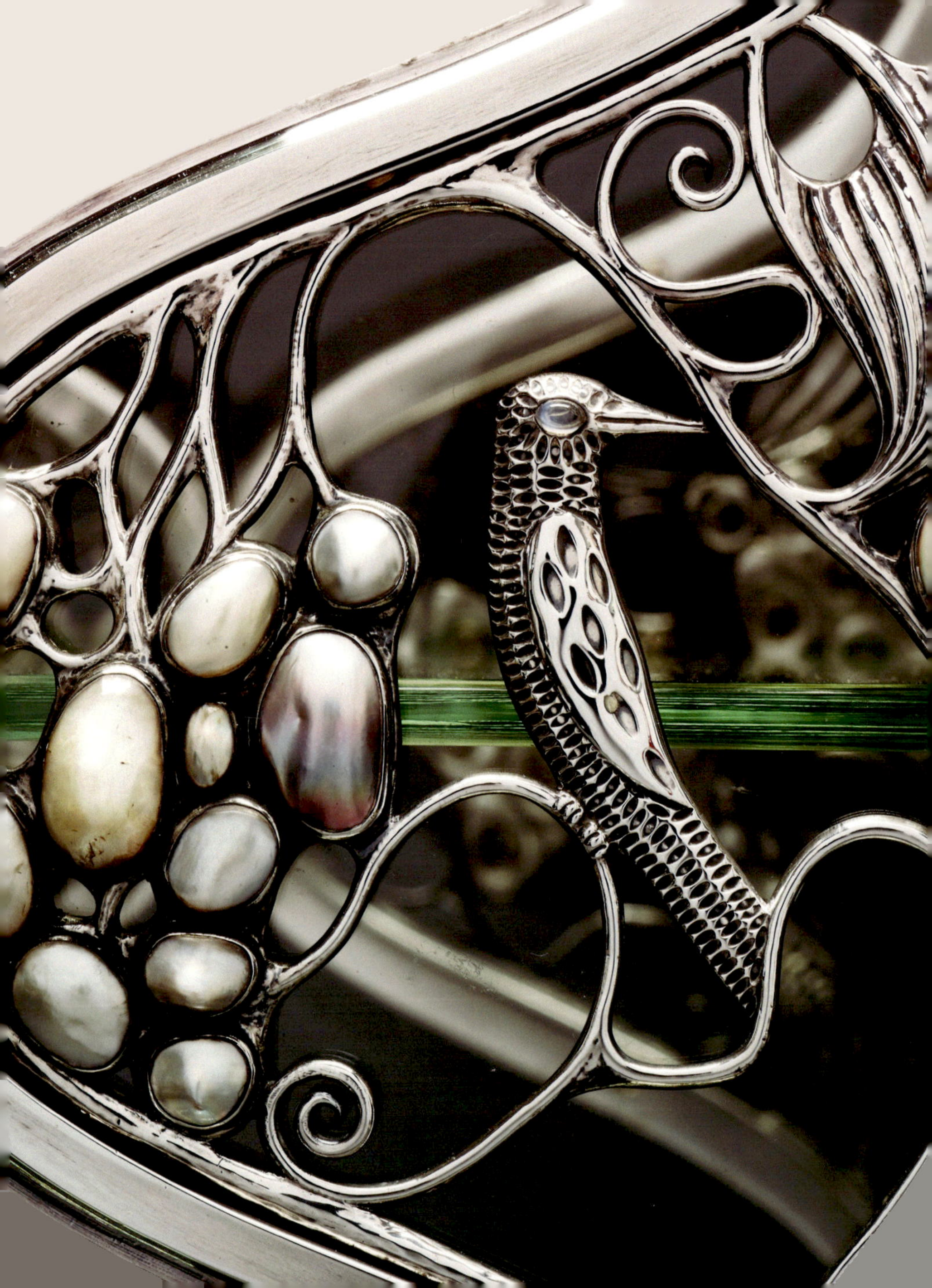

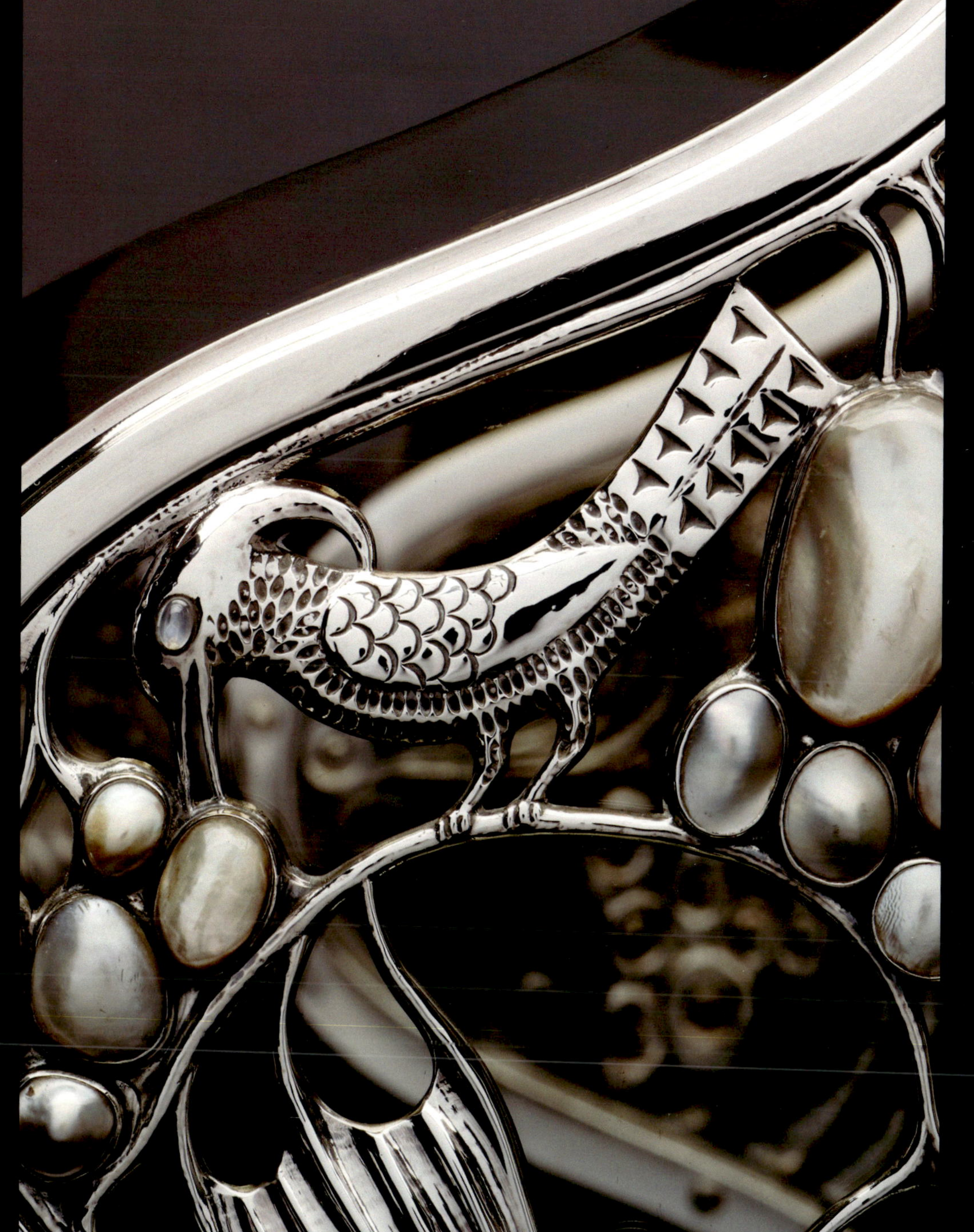

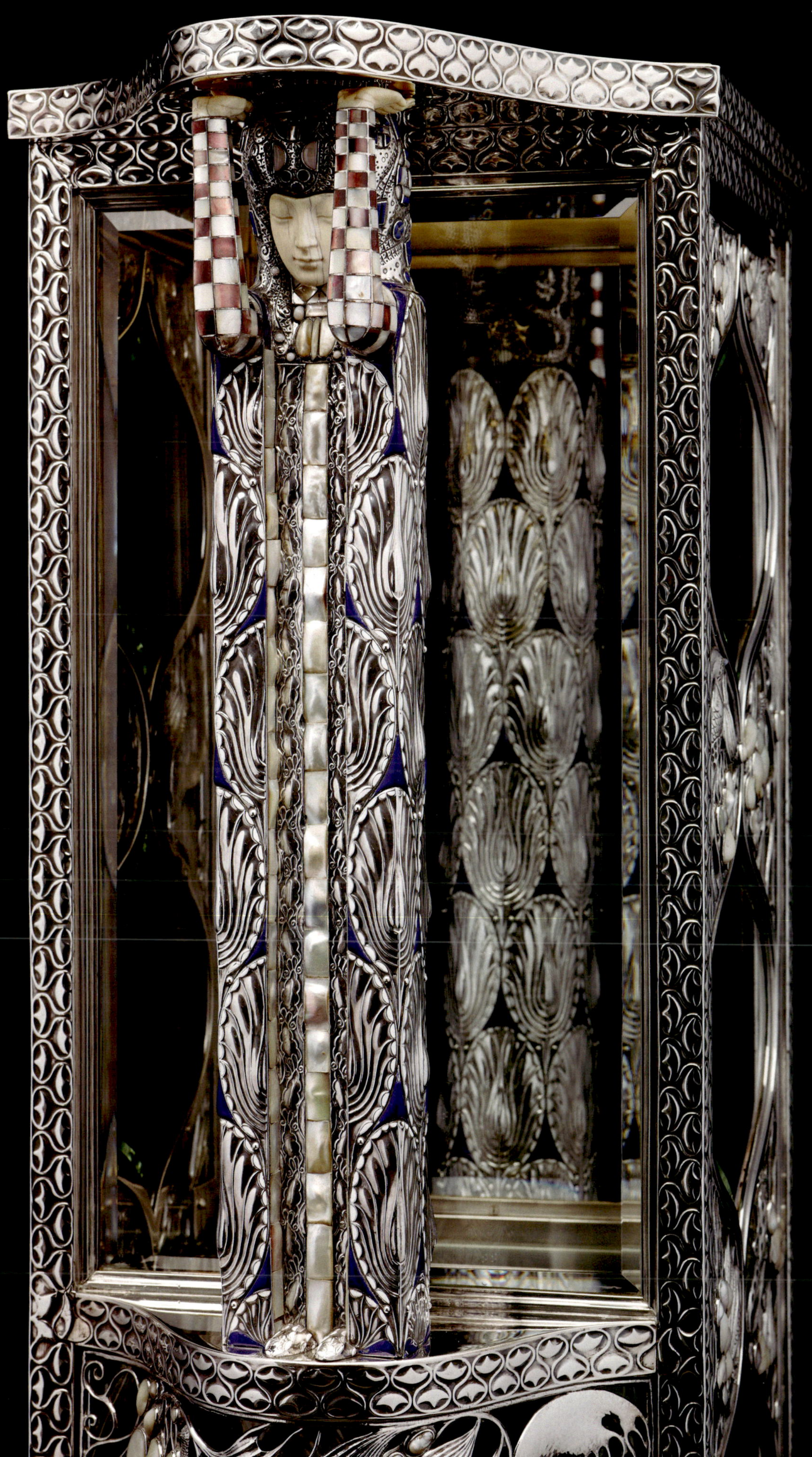

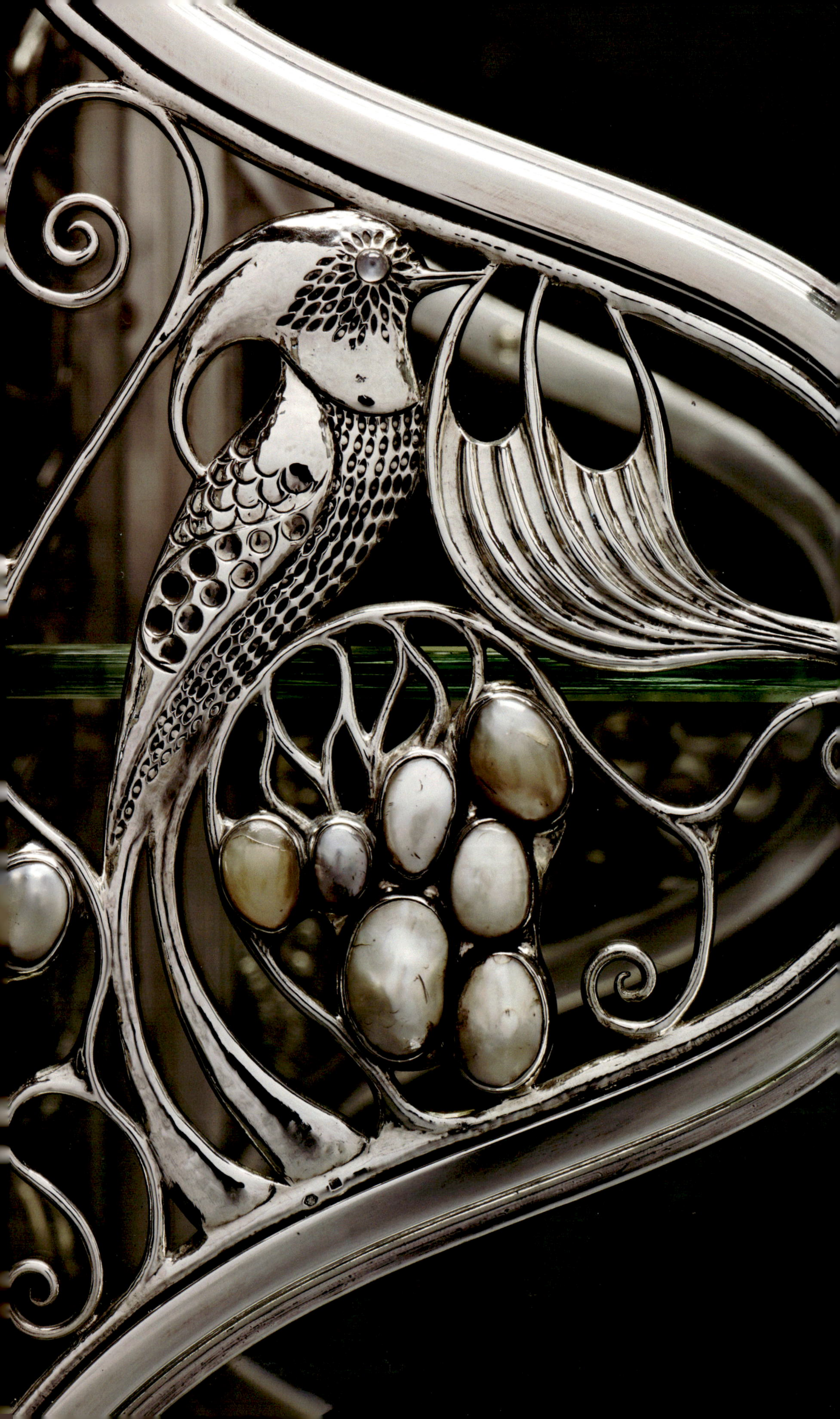

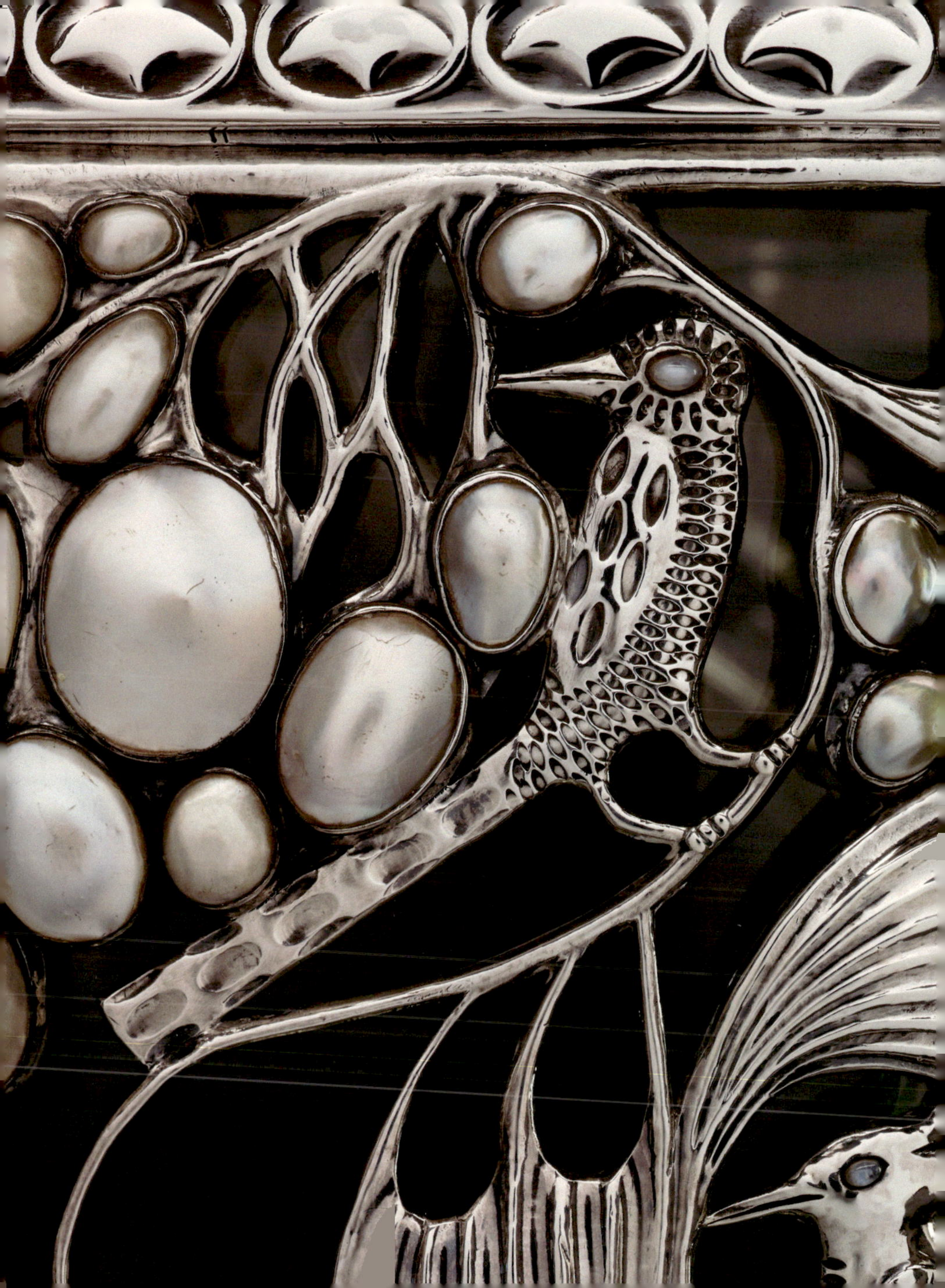

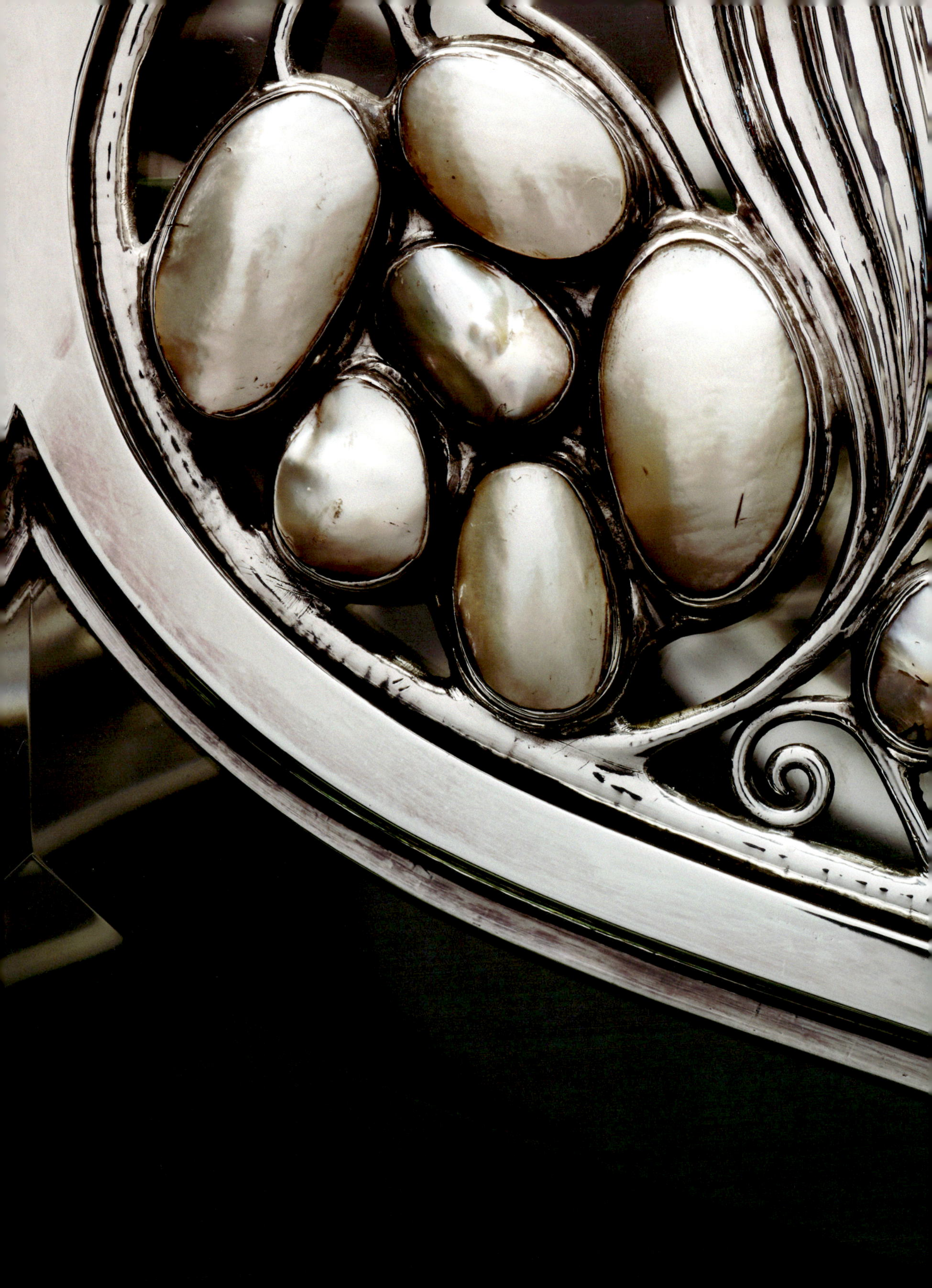

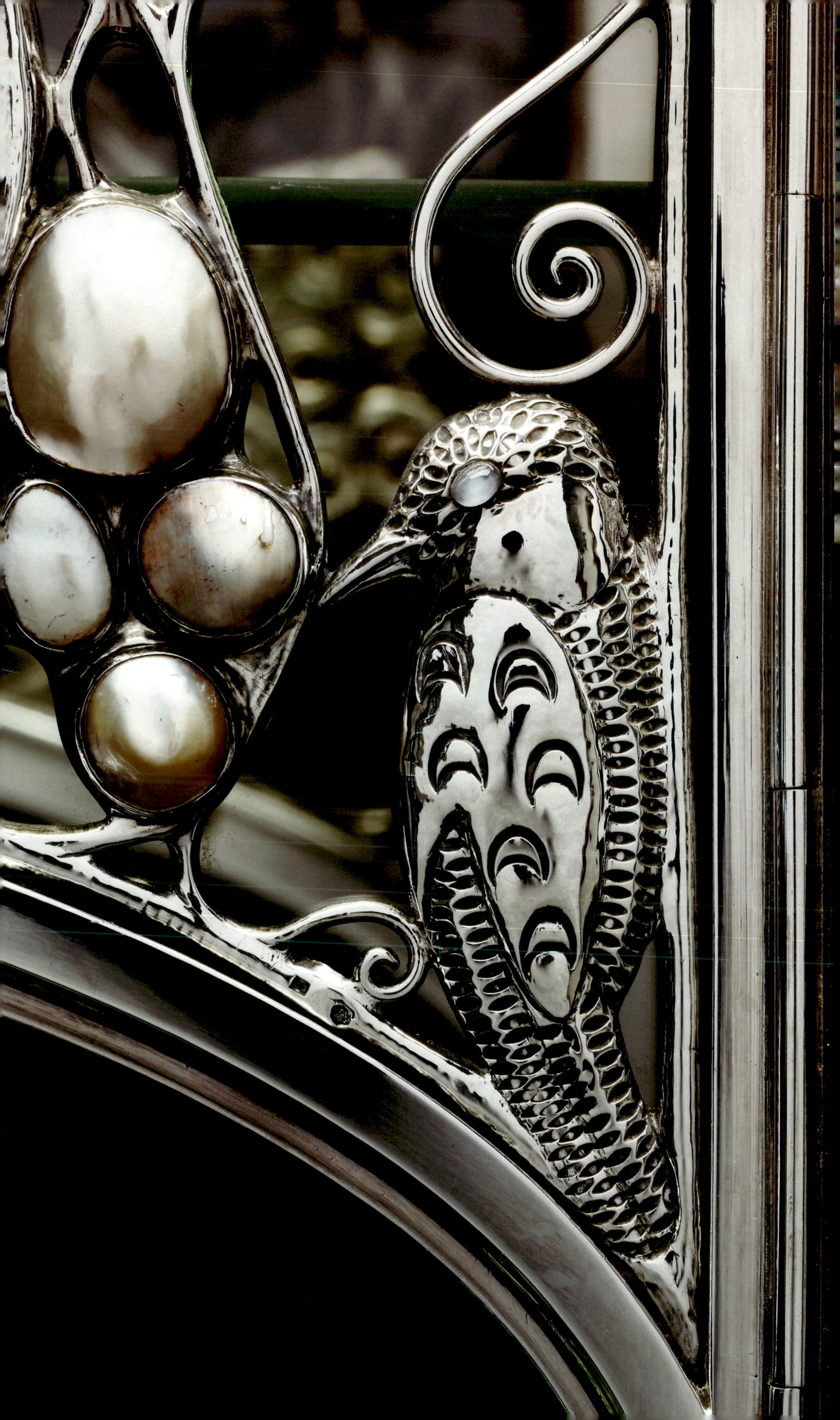

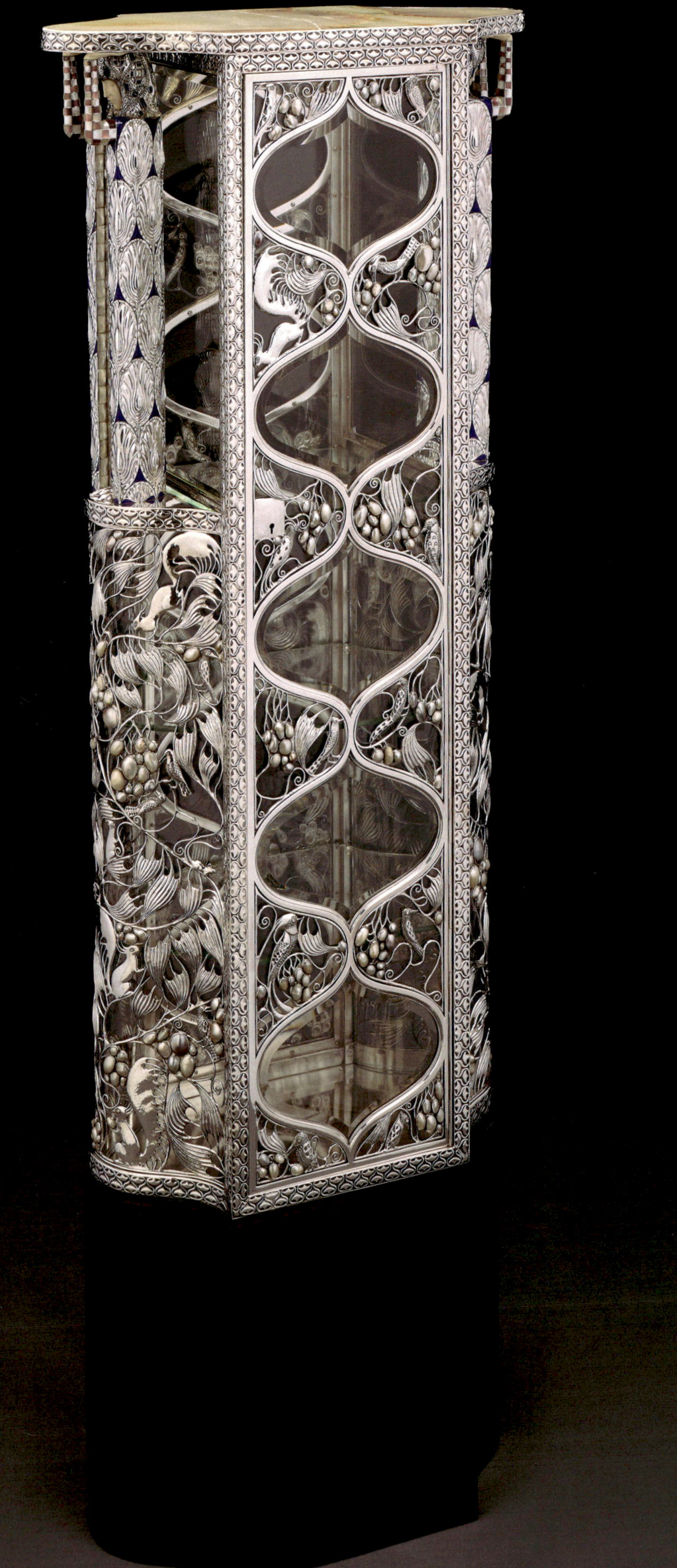

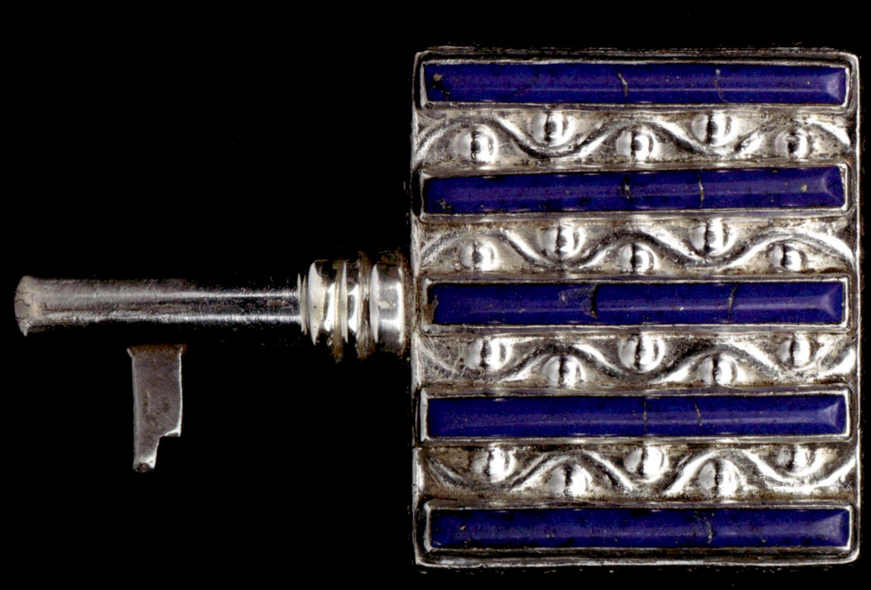

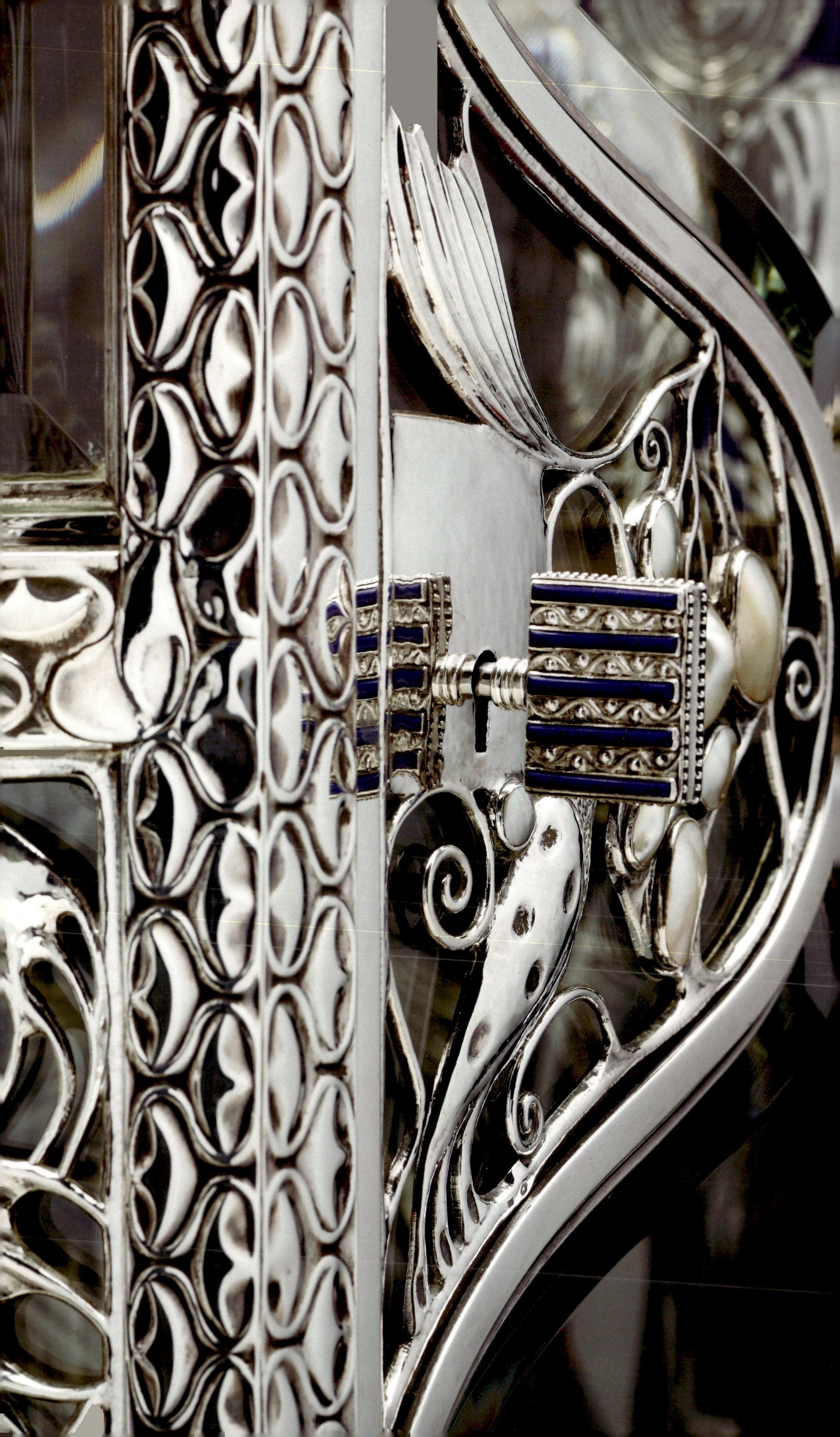

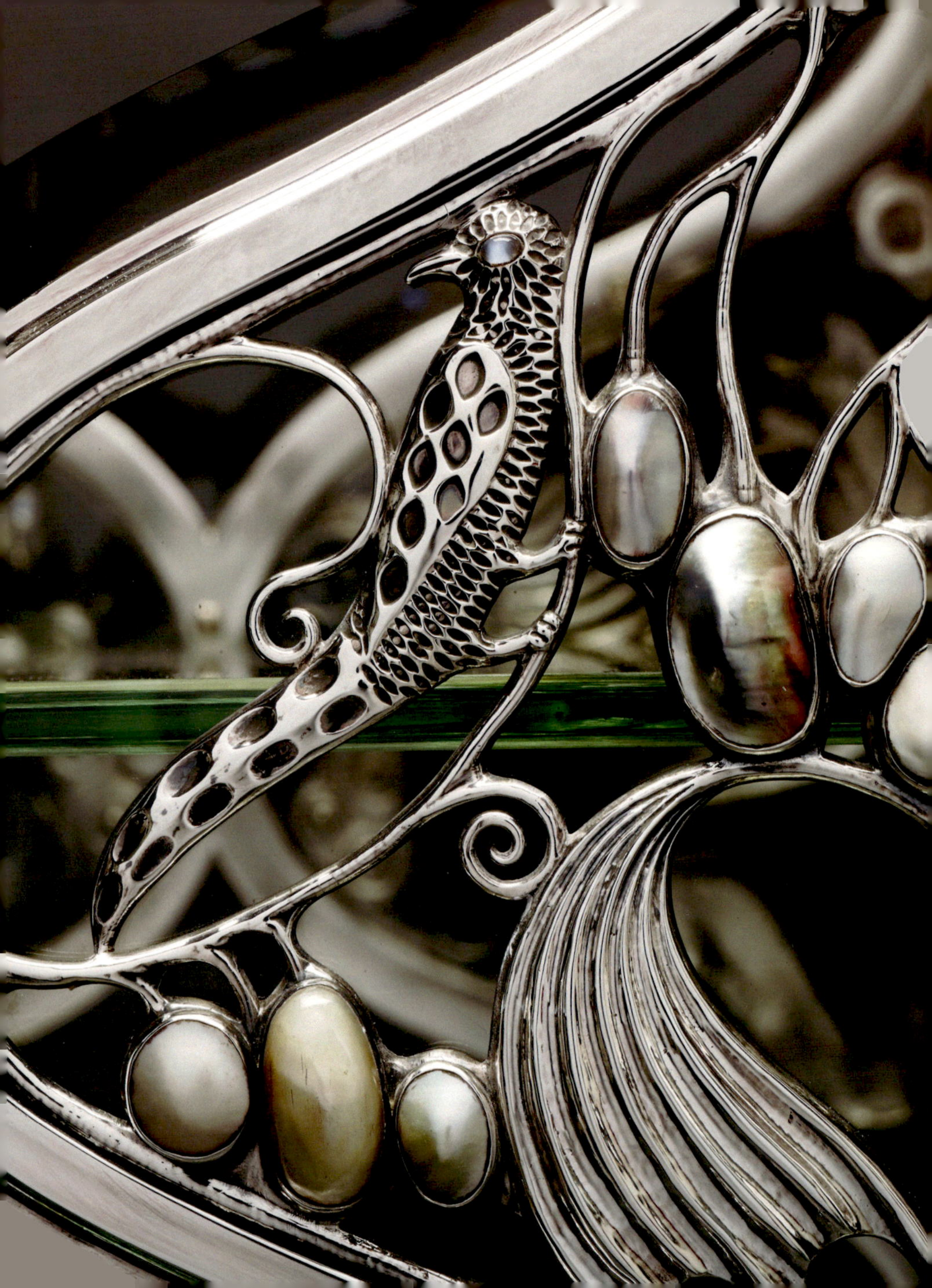

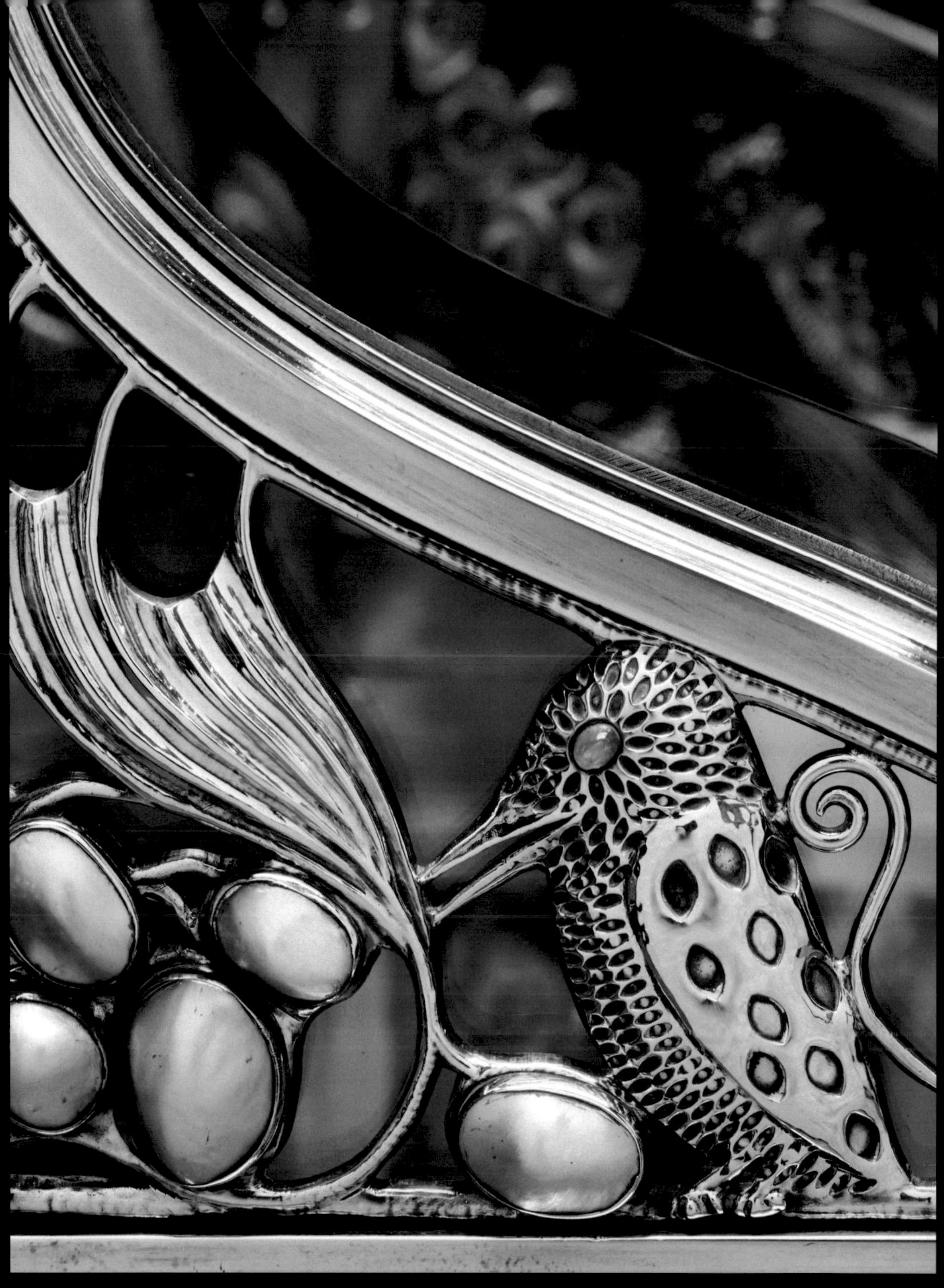

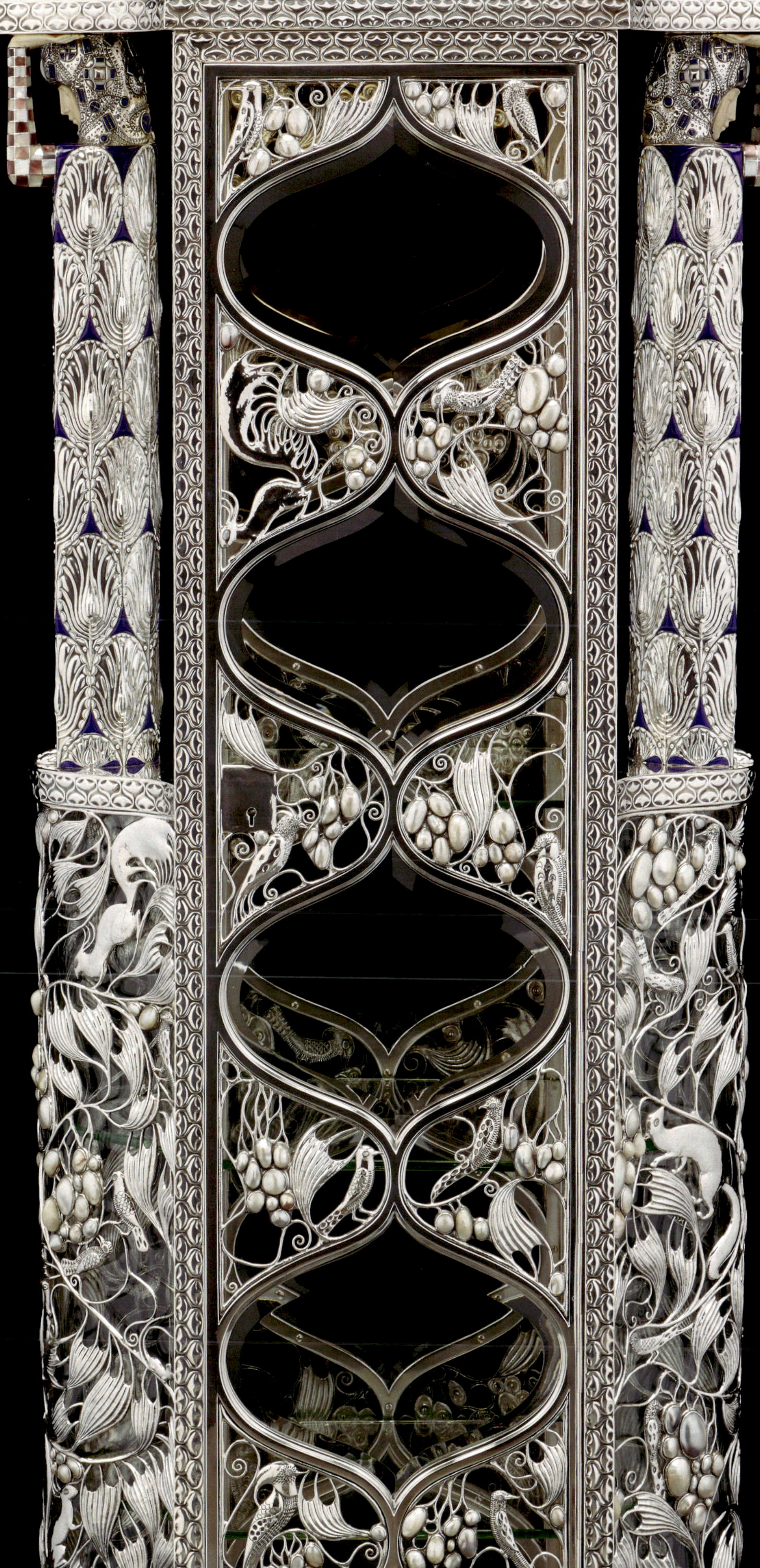

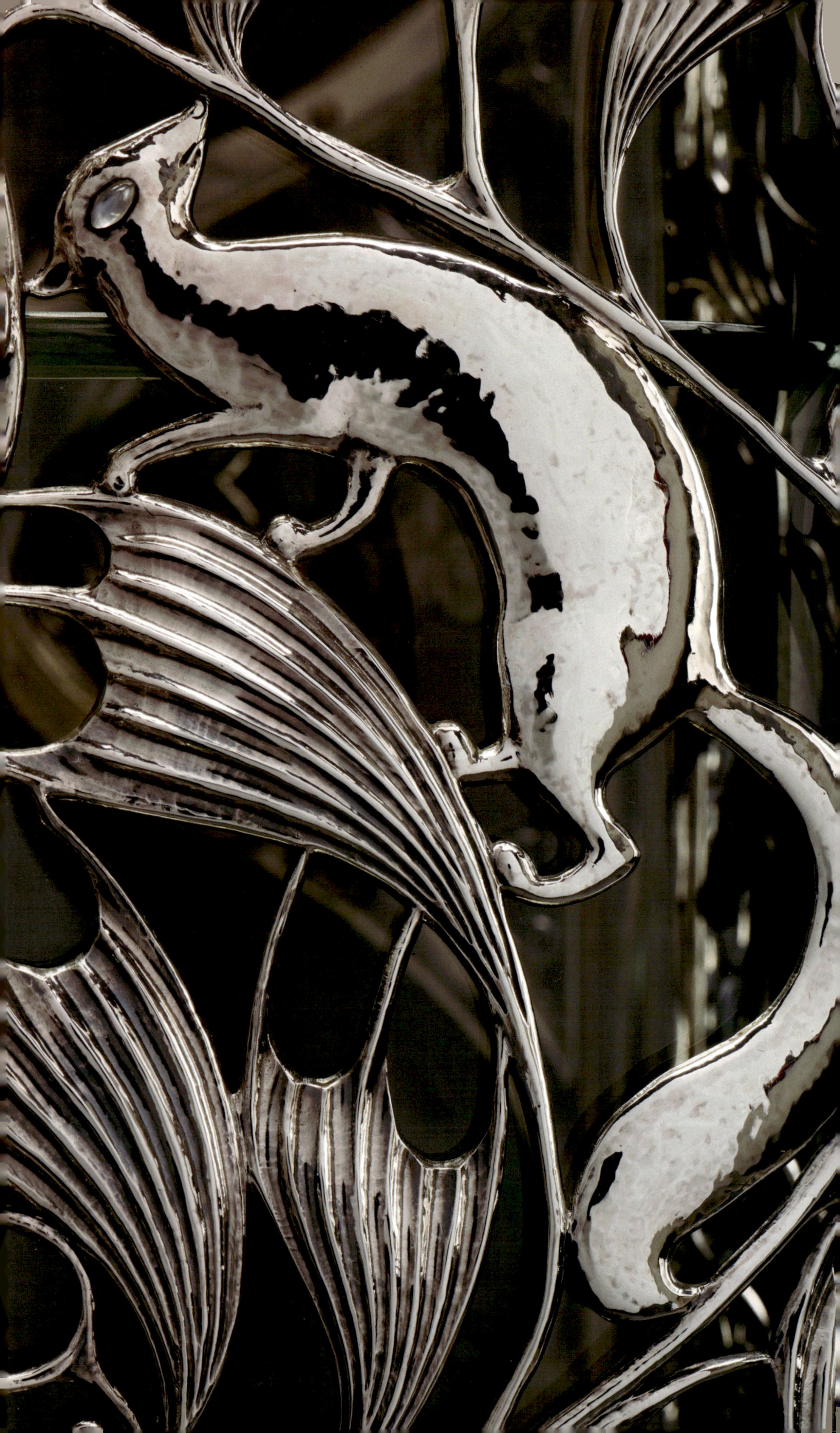

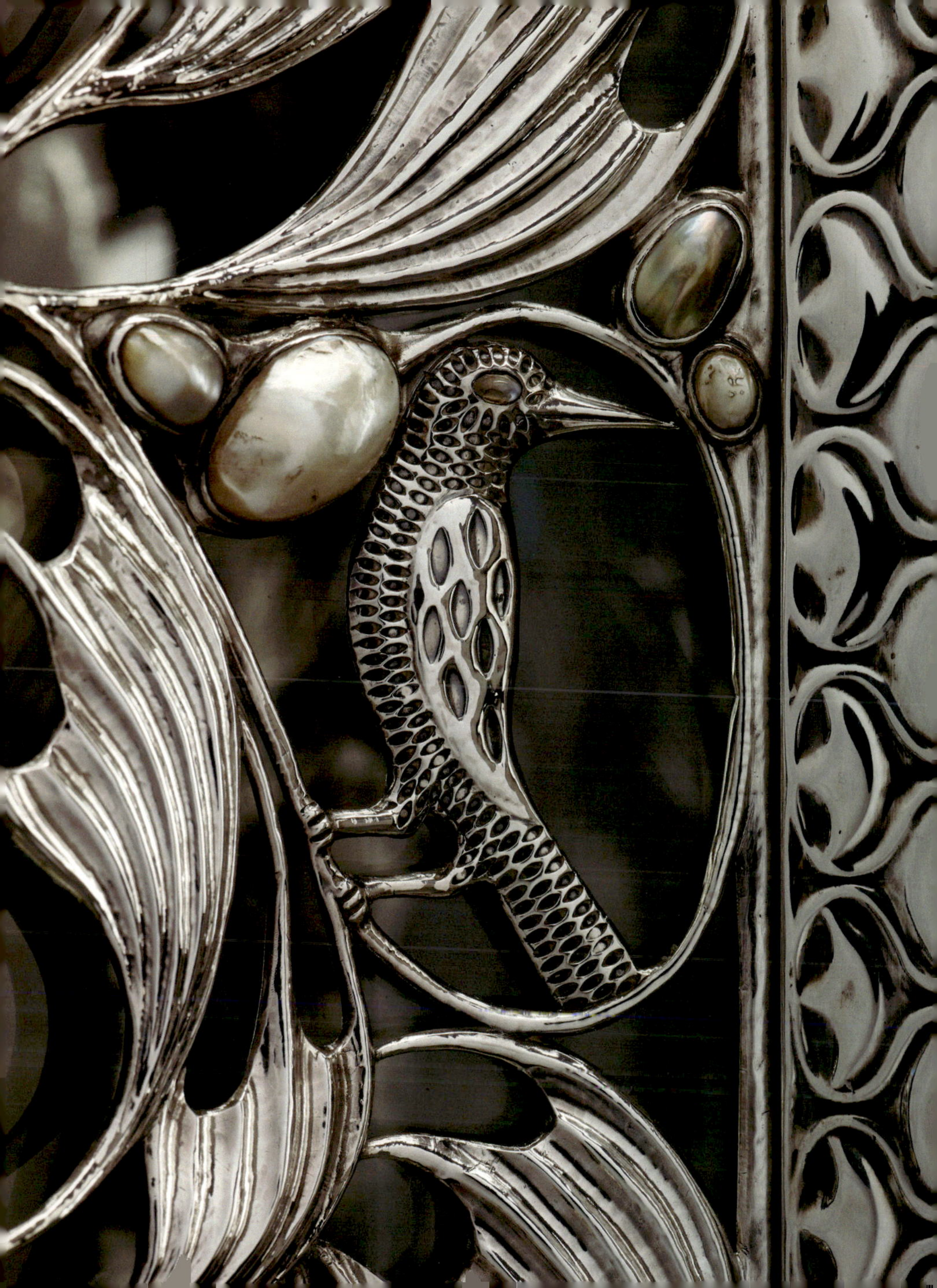

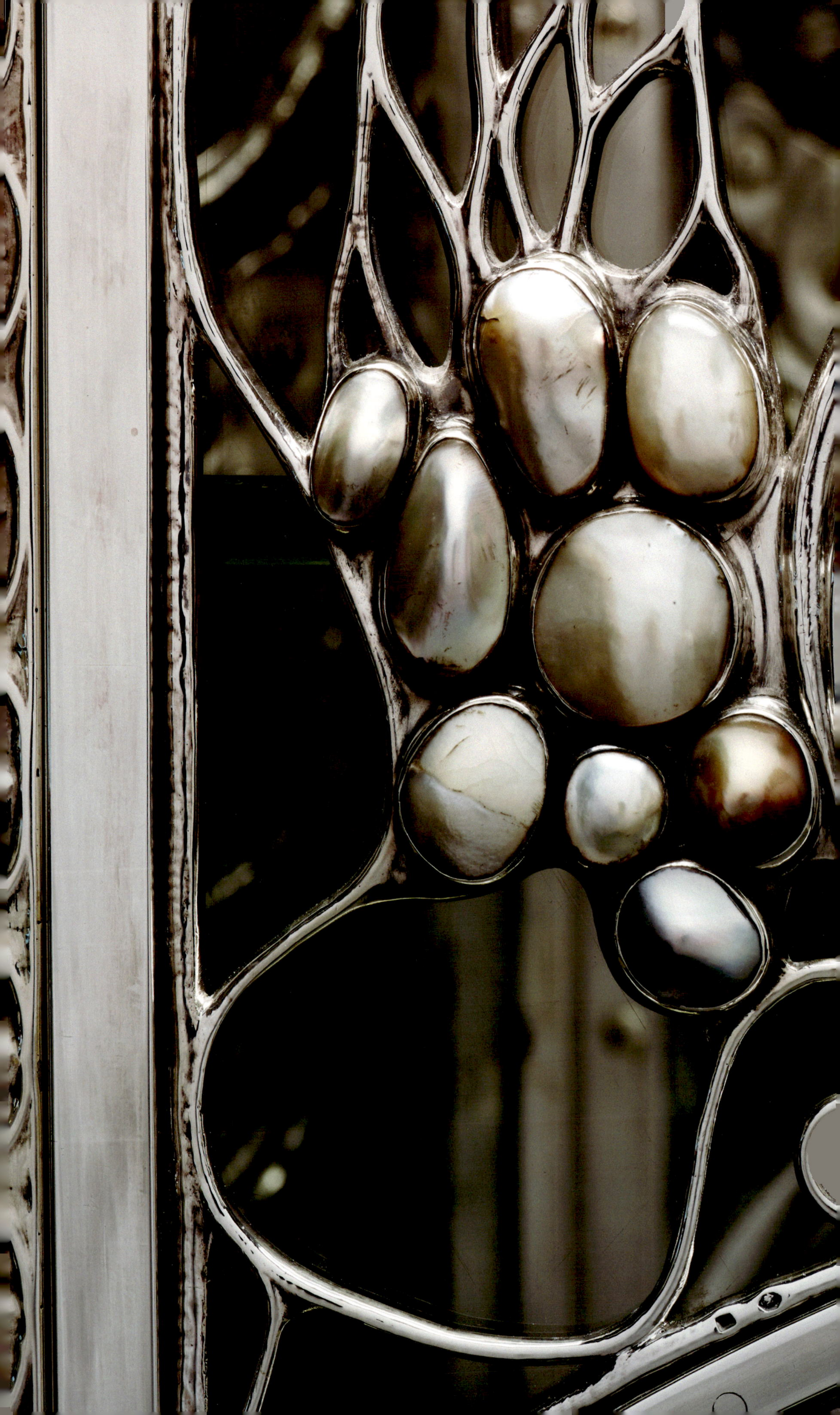

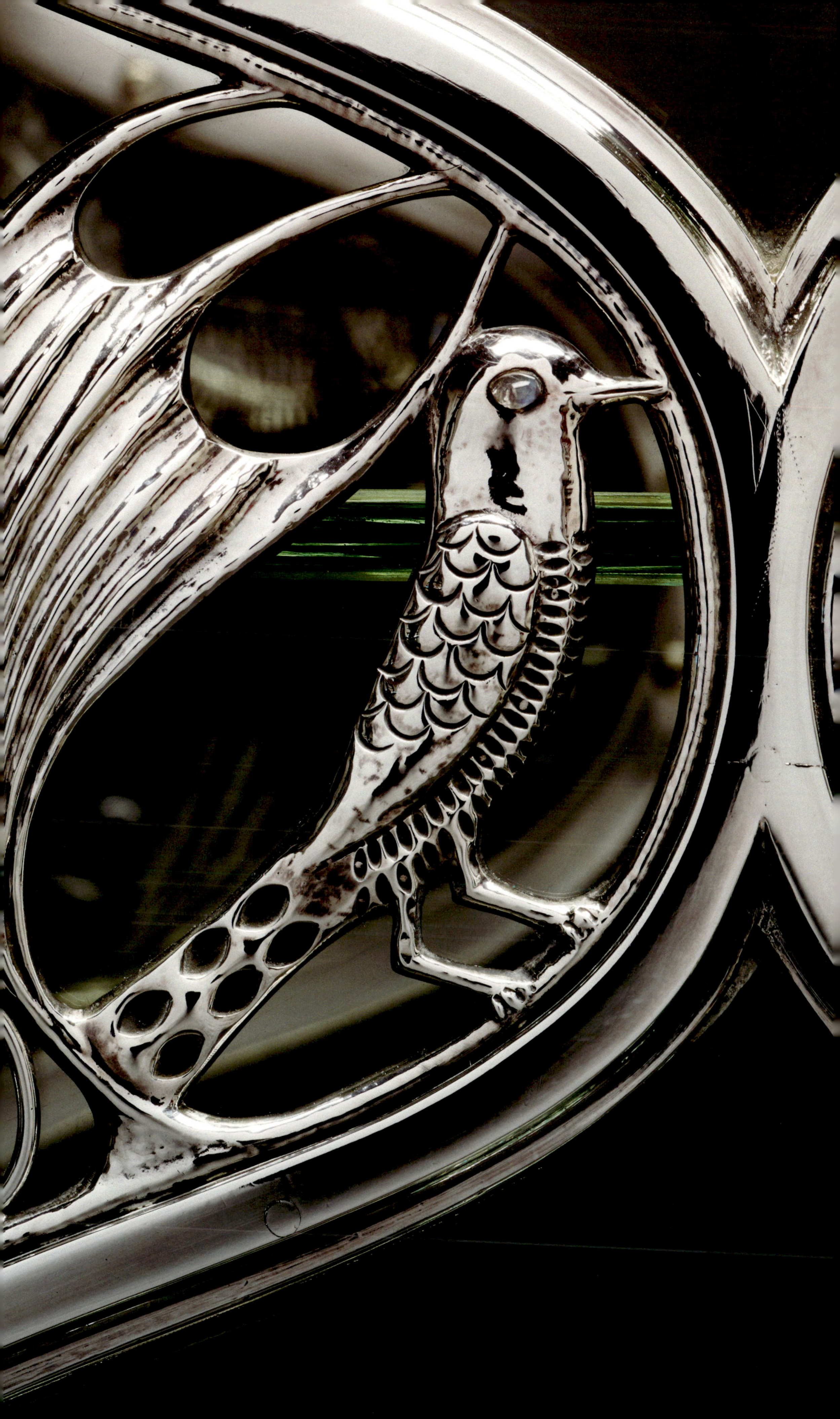

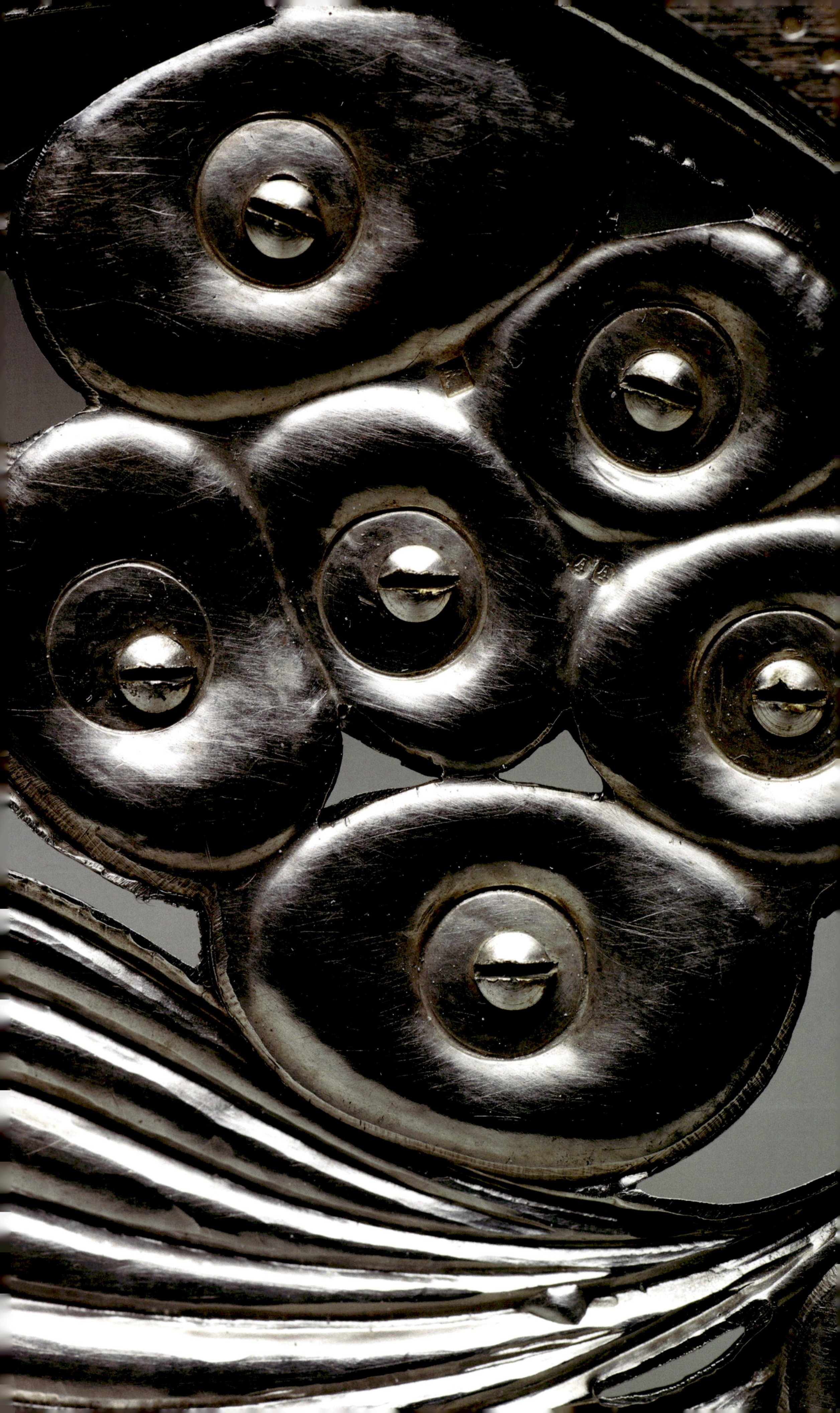

A LOOK INSIDE

THE CONSERVATION, STUDY, AND TREATMENT OF THE WITTGENSTEIN VITRINE

FRAN BAAS

In the fall of 2013, the Dallas Museum of Art acquired a stunning silver vitrine, dating to 1908, that had been designed by Carl Otto Czeschka and made in Vienna by the Wiener Werkstätte—a collaborative group of artists, architects, and designers founded there in 1903. The vitrine, or display cabinet, had originally been owned by the Wittgenstein family of Vienna and is the largest and most lavish example known of the silverwork designed and executed by the Werkstätte. A triumph of early twentieth-century design, it is made almost entirely of silver and decorated with baroque pearls, semiprecious stones, such as opals, moonstones, onyx, and lapis lazuli, and ivory, mother-of-pearl, and enamel. Still stunning more than a hundred years after it had been made, the vitrine was, nonetheless, in need of cleaning and repair (figs. 44 and 45). A large and complex piece (it stands 70 inches high and is 24 inches wide), it required a multidisciplinary approach to treatment. Each of the component materials presented its own problems, and each required a different solution (fig. 46).

After six months on display for a short preliminary exhibition, the vitrine was moved to the DMA's photography studio (fig. 47), where a complete set of photographs of the untreated piece was made (fig. 48). This is an important step in any conservation treatment because it allows conservators to document and monitor the condition of an object. The vitrine was then moved to the Objects Conservation Lab for thorough examination, technical study, and conservation treatment. Armed with the results of the initial examination, the curatorial and conservation staff discussed the overarching goal of the treatment, namely, to bring the piece as close as possible to its original appearance in 1908 (fig. 49).

Because the vitrine is so complex, in both its construction and its condition, the conservation department needed to spend a considerable period of time studying and then treating it, time that would permit us to become familiar with the piece and expand on our knowledge of the Werkstätte's practice. The numerous problems with the

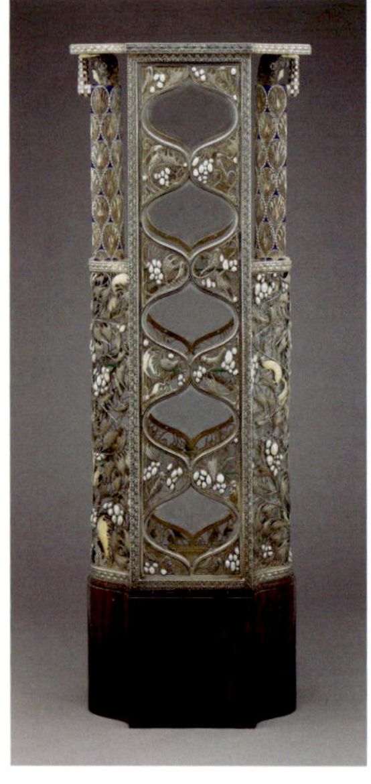

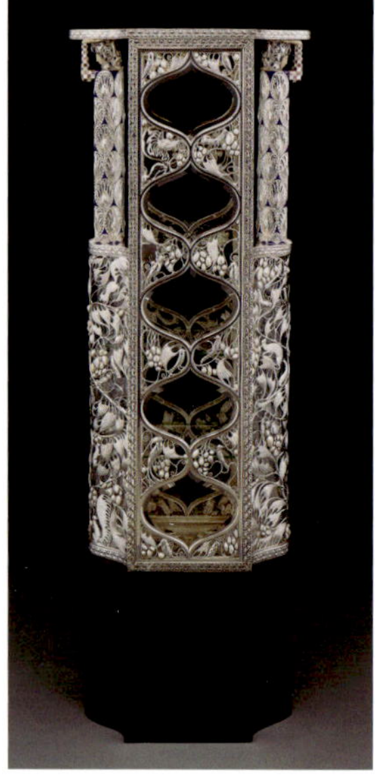

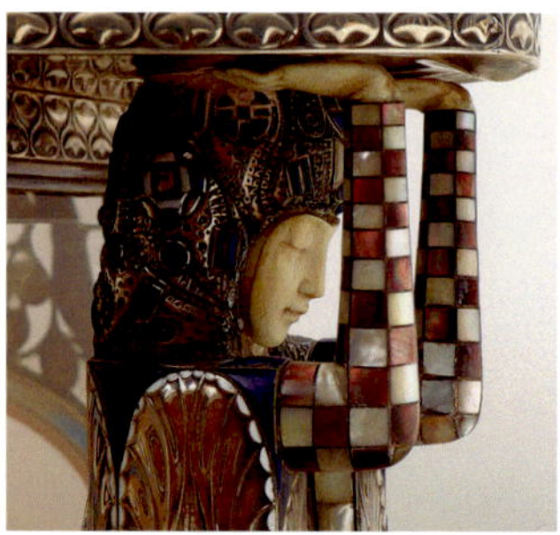

FIGURE 44 The Wittgenstein vitrine when it arrived at the Dallas Museum of Art in the fall of 2013 and before treatment was begun.

FIGURE 45 The vitrine in the fall of 2014, after conservation.

FIGURE 46 Detail of one of the caryatid figures on the vitrine, showing the variety of materials used: semiprecious stones, such as opals and lapis lazuli, and ivory, mother-of-pearl, and enamel.

condition of the piece, the collaborative nature of the project, and the opportunity to study the vitrine thoroughly while we were treating it, made this an ideal focus for an exhibition to be held in the Museum's new Conservation Gallery, a space intended, in presenting an explanation and display of the processes of technical research and conservation, to engage the public in this aspect of the Museum's work.

The various and complex needs of this object required the expertise of not only the conservation staff in the Museum, but also other restorers and conservators who had specific experience in treating the different materials. And, notwithstanding the scope of the project, we had only nine months before the exhibition was scheduled to open in the Conservation Gallery. Therefore, we needed to determine treatment priorities and set weekly goals for all the players if we were to meet our deadline. As with any large, in-depth treatment, interesting discoveries were made along the way—all contributing to an understanding of the history of the piece, of the artisans, and of the overall historical context.

CONDITION BEFORE TREATMENT

The vitrine came to the Museum having been in the collections of only a few previous owners, and their love and care throughout the years for this masterpiece was evident. Unfortunately, this care was apparent in the form of silver polish residue, lurking in every crevice and indentation,

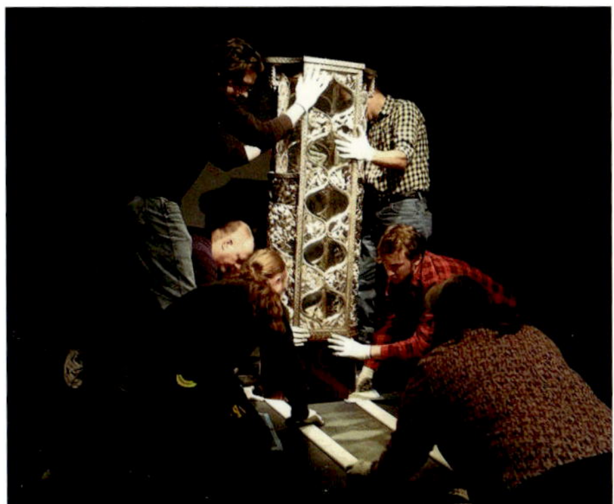

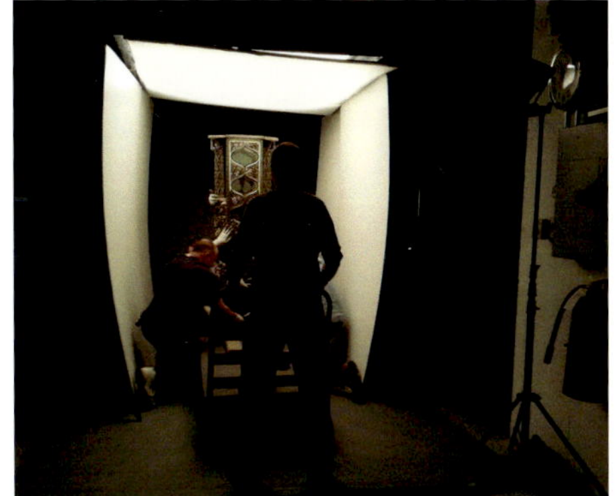

FIGURE 47 DMA preparation staff removing the vitrine from the galleries after a short exhibition.

FIGURE 48 The vitrine was moved to the DMA photography studio, where a complete set of digital photographs was made to document the condition before treatment.

FIGURE 49 Curatorial and conservation staff discussing treatment goals.

FIGURE 50 Detail, showing the Imperial Austro-Hungarian government's *Dianakopf* (Diana's Head) stamp, used by the assayer to document the quality of silver in the vitrine. Within the hexagonal shape of the stamp, the following marks can be seen: the head of the goddess Diana (characterized by the crescent moon on her headdress); on the left, the number 2 which, along with the hexagonal shape, indicates the level of purity (in this case, 90 percent silver); and, on the right, the letter A, which signifies that the piece was made in Vienna.

FIGURE 51 Drawings of assay stamps used to indicate varying percentages of silver in the stamped objects, the percentages ranging from 75 percent to 95 percent. These stamps do not include any indication of the place of manufacture, such as the A, for Vienna, to be found on the stamp on the vitrine (see figure 50).

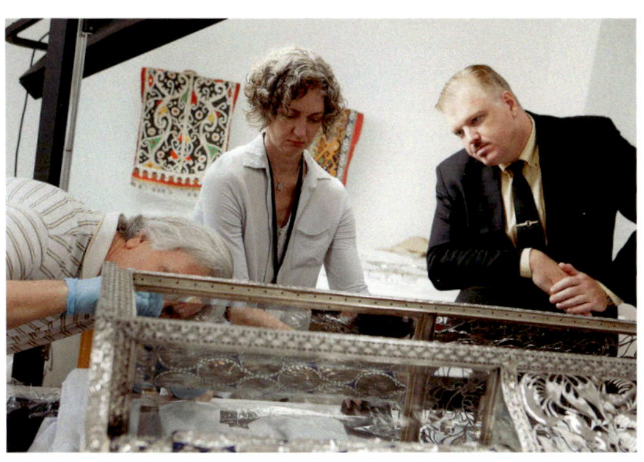

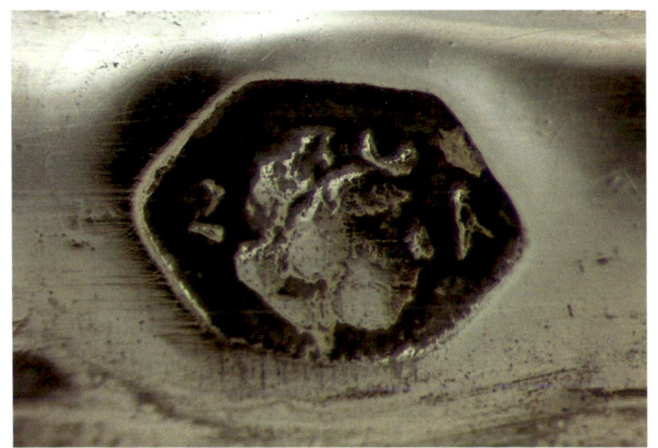

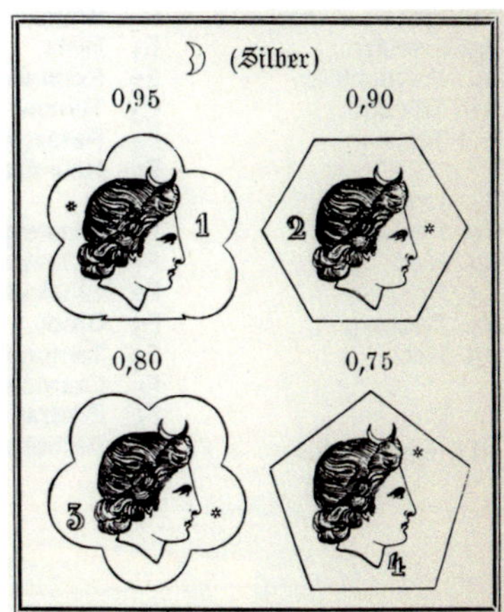

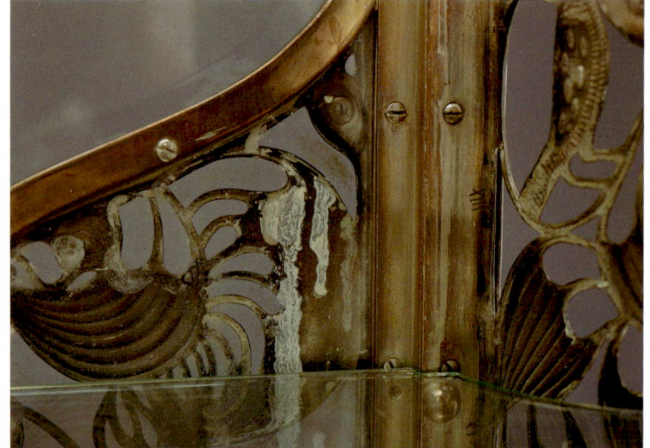

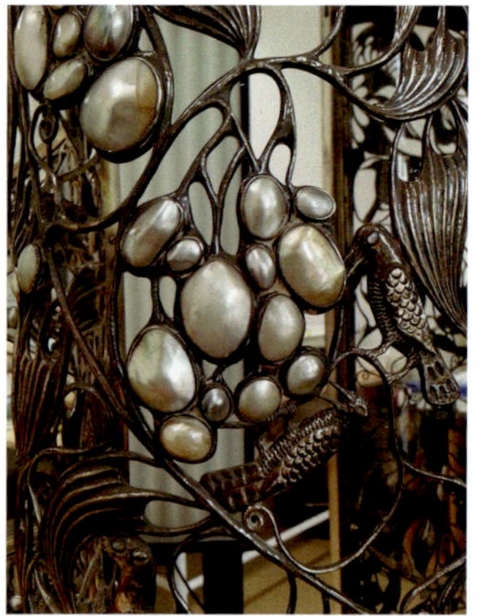

FIGURE 52 Detail, showing polish residue trapped between the glass and the back of the silver elements.

FIGURE 53 Detail of the clusters of baroque pearls and the intricacy of the silver setting that has been darkened with tarnish and residual polish.

trapped between the silver elements and the inside glass panes, and impossible to remove without completely dismantling the vitrine (figs. 52 and 53). Additionally, one of the curved glass side panels was entirely missing and the wooden base had been extensively altered. Long before the DMA acquired the piece, shipment damage must have caused or exacerbated many of the problems we found, such as the cracked or missing glass, the cracked onyx gemstone top, and the large dent along the edge of the top silver tray supporting the onyx. There were also instances of lesser damage, such as mother-of-pearl tiles that were loose.

TECHNICAL ANALYSIS

Analytical techniques help provide information about objects being treated and shed light on specific materials, techniques used by the artist or workshop, provenance, and authenticity. Aside from the simple microscope, we now have access to other instruments, and can often combine multiple resources in making a treatment plan. The techniques in the conservator's proverbial diagnostic toolbox range from simple, visual observation under different lighting sources (from various energies on the electromagnetic spectrum and at different degrees of magnification) to the analysis of chemical properties using various specialized instruments. At the Dallas Museum of Art we can perform X-ray fluorescence (XRF) analysis, which is a nondestructive technique for determining the presence of various elements in the materials used. Not only is the information gained by this technique useful for the curator, but also it can help guide treatment decisions. In this project, spectra were gathered from two different inorganic materials, the silver and the glass. The other materials could be identified visually because they are so distinctive.

SILVER

The results of the XRF analysis for the silver were not unusual: they all suggested that the vitrine was made of a high-quality silver alloy.[1] Pure silver is too soft to be used for something of this nature. Artworks or jewelry made of precious metals are frequently hallmarked (depending on the legal requirements of the area in which they were made) and the metal content is analyzed or assayed for what is called its "claim to fineness." The official assayer's mark (in this case, the Austro-Hungarian government's *Dianakopf* stamp, figs. 50 and 51 on p. 69) can be seen on each separate silver element in the vitrine. With the aid of a stereomicroscope, the stamp reveals important historical information about location of manufacture and quality of silver. Within the hexagonal shape of the mark on the vitrine, the following marks can be seen: the head of the goddess Diana (characterized by the crescent moon on her headdress), the number 2, which indicates the level of purity (90 percent silver), and the letter *A*, which signifies that the piece was made in Vienna. The assayer's mark notwithstanding, the XRF spectra taken from the decorative silver elements indicated that the degree of purity was higher and, in some parts, exceeded that of sterling, which is 92.5 percent silver. Impurities of gold, lead, and bismuth were to be found in most of the silver, and the alloy was not uniform, but even this is not unusual, as the object is handmade. The main structural silver elements also contained arsenic—most likely added for work hardening (that is, to improve strength and hardness).

GLASS

The results of the XRF analysis determined that the glass used throughout the vitrine was a soda-lime glass, the most common form. This is composed of silica, sodium oxide, calcium oxide (lime), and other minor additives. What was particularly interesting was the presence of arsenic. Research led to the discovery that arsenious oxide was often added to molten glass, resulting in glass that is not only very clear but also very sturdy.

MINERALS

Visual observations of the minerals and gemstones were made under both visible and ultraviolet light and confirmed the earlier identification of these decorations that had been made when the vitrine first arrived at the Museum.[2] The different materials display different visible characteristics—moonstones, for example, display a chatoyancy in visible light,[3] and opals have an iridescent haze in visible light and appear milky under long-wave ultraviolet light. (Under long-wave ultraviolet light that falls within the range from 320 to 400 nm, different materials exhibit different fluorescent colors indicating the presence of particular materials or revealing aspects not visible to the naked eye, such as restorations.) Mother-of-pearl fluoresces brightly under long-wave ultraviolet light. On one of the caryatid's arms there are two small tiles that are restorations (painted to look like pearl) that can easily be spotted under ultraviolet light because they do not fluoresce. This discovery was both interesting and useful, as it confirmed the supposition that the vitrine had toppled over, damaging several areas in the process.

TREATMENT

SILVER

The most aesthetically important, if most time-consuming, part of the treatment was the reduction of the tarnish and the old polish residue (some was left for definition). Because the piece was so big and consisted of so much silver and because the designs were so intricate and complex, each section had to be dismantled. Tarnish consists of black silver sulfide and is caused by the off-gassing of sulfur-containing compounds that are present in our air as a result of the burning of fossil fuels. These sulfurous compounds are also commonly found in our everyday environment, in such things as wool, some foam rubbers, carpet padding, and some paints. Silver molecules combine with the off-gassing compounds to produce the corrosion product we call tarnish. The exterior of the vitrine had most likely been polished regularly, and it had a lighter layer of tarnish. The interior, relatively inaccessible, surfaces were almost black from tarnish. The disfiguring layer of tarnish had to be reduced, since part of the beauty of the piece is the transparency of the clear glass combined with the shimmering silver. The old polish residues, which had built up on the back of the silver parts and within interstices and corners, also diminished the essential transparency of the piece. The first treatment step, therefore, was the mechanical removal of the polish residue with a soft brush and cotton swabs (fig. 54).

Several commonly used techniques were considered for cleaning the tarnish, among them, polishing, chemical dips, and electrochemical reduction. The method chosen for this project was guided not only by the size and complexity of the vitrine but also by standard and approved conservation methods. Submersion and chemical dips were not appropriate for our large and composite object, decorated as it was with a complex variety of materials including ivory, enamel, pearls, glass, and gems, some of which would have been damaged in the process, and because it was so constructed that there were hollow recesses in the main upright supports.

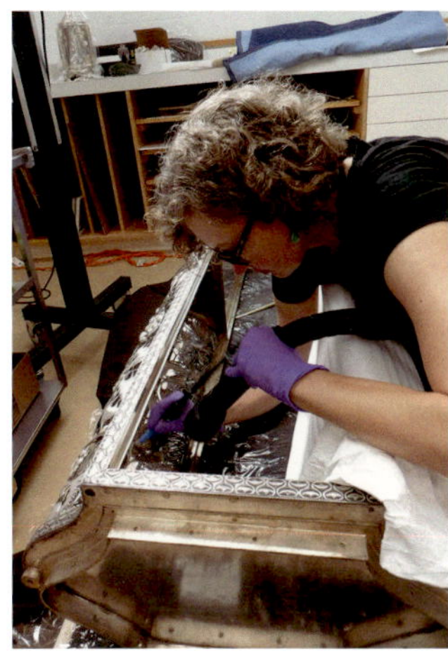

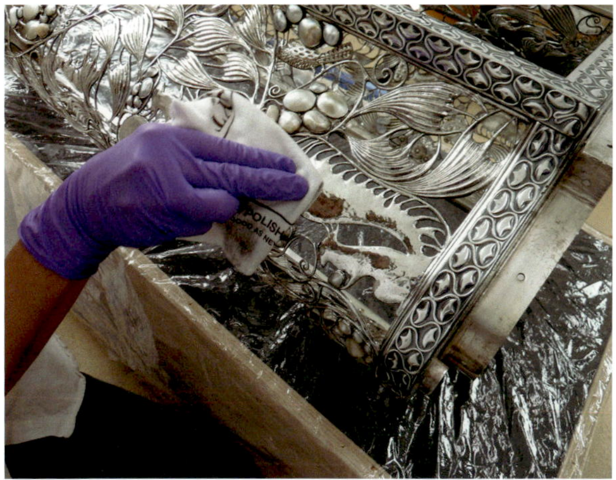

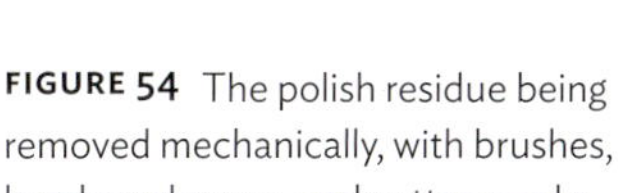

FIGURE 54 The polish residue being removed mechanically, with brushes, bamboo skewers, and cotton swabs.

FIGURE 55 Cleaned polished silver-work being buffed with a soft cloth.

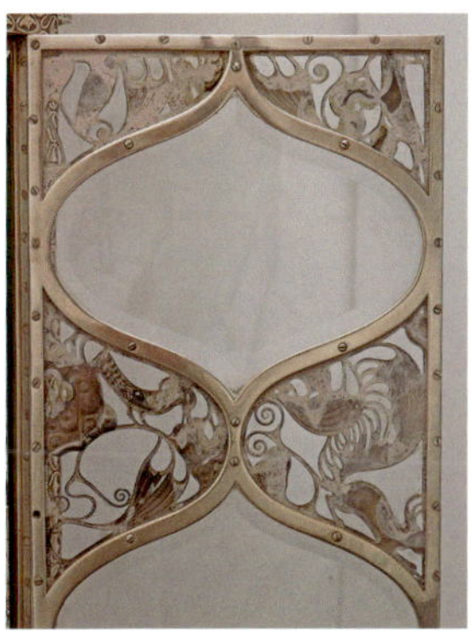

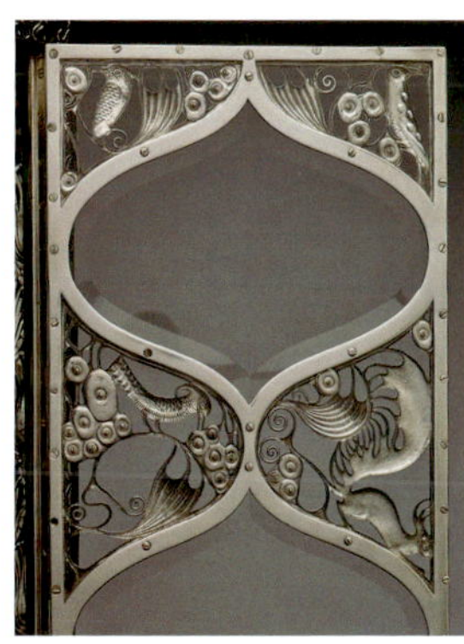

FIGURES 56 AND 57 Interior face of the front door panel before and after treatment. As in a stained-glass window, the glass is held in place by a traditional glazier's putty, and the support framework, under the silver tracery and invisible from the front, is secured by multiple screws.

Choosing the safest and most effective approach, we polished the entire silver body by hand. Conservators do not often use commercial products, as they may contain corrosive chemicals such as ammonia, acids, or harsh abrasives that can permanently damage delicate surfaces. Depending on the chemical composition of the commercial product, which may not be completely divulged on the label, a delicate silver surface can become pitted—leaving more surface area to tarnish and causing the tarnish to reappear more rapidly and be more difficult to remove. For this piece we chose to use a homemade polish slurry made out of precipitated calcium carbonate in water and ethanol. Precipitated calcium carbonate was used because the particle size and shape are more tightly controlled. Once each piece was polished, it was rinsed and given a final wipe with a soft Selvyt cloth[4] to buff the metal and remove stray particles of dust (fig. 55).

The front door and the back panel are constructed like stained-glass windows, held together with hundreds of silver screws (figs. 56 and 57). These panels had to be removed from the main structure so that they could be cleaned on all sides. Every screw and component was identified so that the vitrine could be reassembled as it was originally. To keep

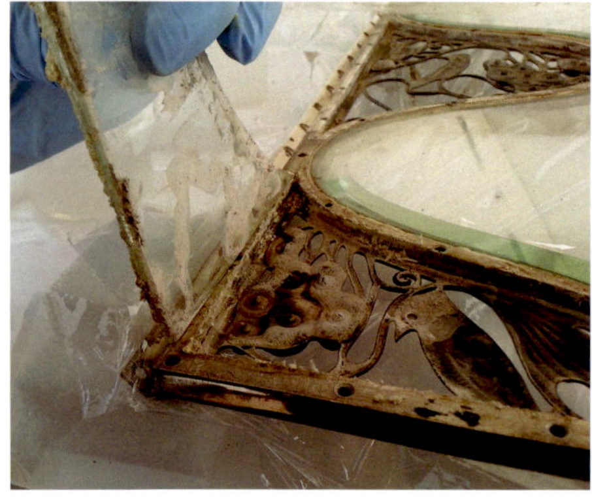

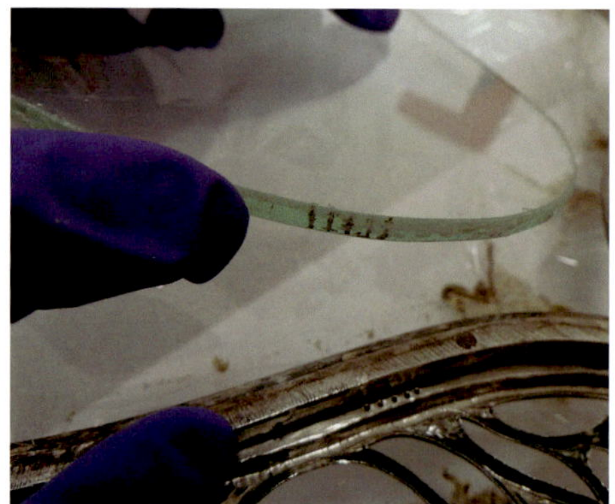

FIGURE 58 Detail of the glass that was held in place in the support framework by glazier's putty. After the putty was removed, the glass panes were taken out and cleaned.

FIGURE 59 Detail showing etched hash marks along the side of the glass pane and corresponding punch marks in the metal of the support framework; these marks were most likely used for registration to ensure that each pane was set in its specific frame.

the hundreds of screws separated and well organized, the collection staff and conservators developed a system of tiny compartments, each mapped to a design key (or diagram). Thus, when it came time to put the pieces back together, each screw, having been individually cleaned with an ultrasonic cleaner and a soft brush, could be returned to its original hole.

The original glazier's putty holding the glass in the framework was softened and removed with a gelled solvent solution.[5] The panes of glass were removed, documented, cleaned, repaired, and set aside (fig. 58). The back of the silver elements could now be accessed and cleaned.

As the piece was dismantled for cleaning, we could see the original methods of registration, that is, the series of marks used by the maker to ensure that the individual elements of a piece will be assembled according to a specific design. Because many artisans with differing specialties were working simultaneously on this project, it would make sense to have a labeling or numbering system for each piece, whether glass and metal. On the thicker metal framework holding the glass in place (under the tracery), small punch marks were made in the metal to correspond to etched score marks along the appropriate cut edge of the small glass panes (fig. 59). This interesting discovery revealed an insight into a method of manufacture that is rarely seen once an object has been completed.

REPAIRING THE DENT

Above the head of one of the caryatids there was a significant dent in the horizontal silver tray (in which the large flat onyx gemstone sits) on the top of the vitrine (figs. 60 and 61). After the onyx had been removed, the screws holding the tray to the upright supports could be undone and the tray itself removed from the vitrine. A silicon cast of the dent was

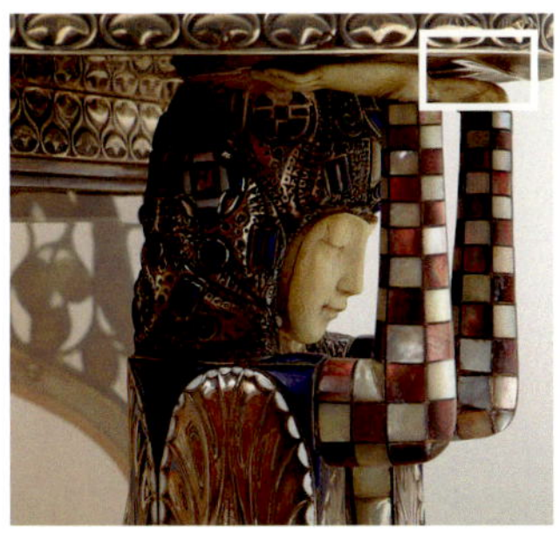

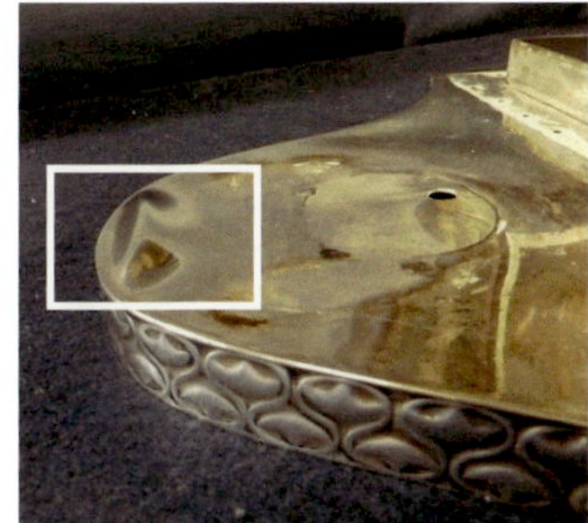

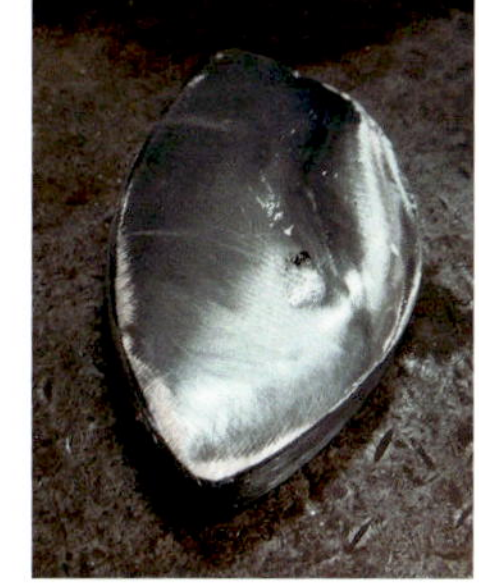

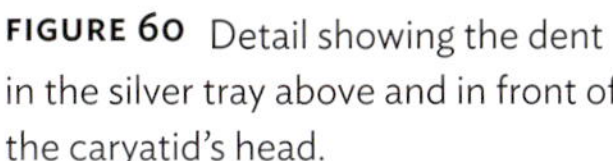

FIGURE 60 Detail showing the dent in the silver tray above and in front of the caryatid's head.

FIGURE 61 Detail showing the silver tray after the onyx was removed, with the dent clearly apparent.

FIGURE 62 A mold of the existing dent made to provide support for the metal while the damage is being repaired.

FIGURE 63 The dent being mechanically massaged out of the silver.

FIGURE 64 Detail of the silver tray after the dent had been removed and the silver polished up.

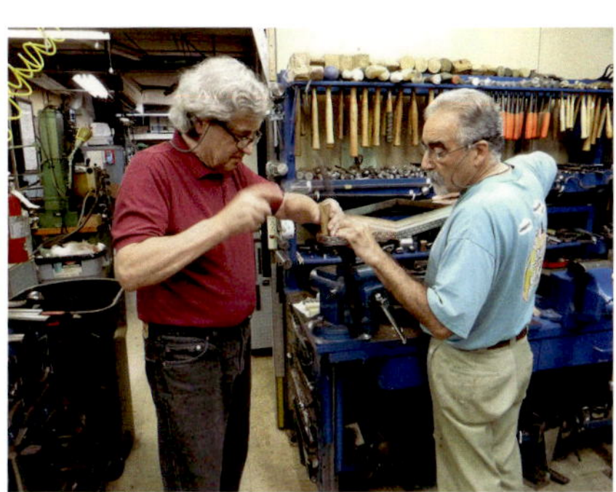

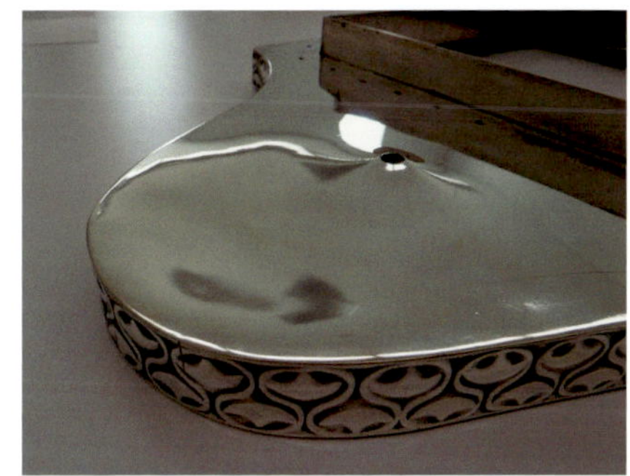

made and, from that, a series of supports, made of different metals and different woods (and thus characterized by a range of varying hardness), and in gradually changing shapes, was fabricated (fig. 62). With the tray balanced on these supports, the dent was gently massaged out with hand tools (which also varied in hardness) (fig. 63) so that the silver molecules would be coaxed back out to their former, more uniform thickness. This was a delicate procedure, as care had to be taken not to damage the join between the flat plate and its decorative lip. Any working marks were then carefully polished out, returning the silver to its original mirrorlike reflective surface (fig. 64).[6]

THE GLASS

Originally, the vitrine had two large curved glass panels running down the inside of each side to close off the interior from the elements. They also increased the reflective quality of the silver. Unfortunately, when

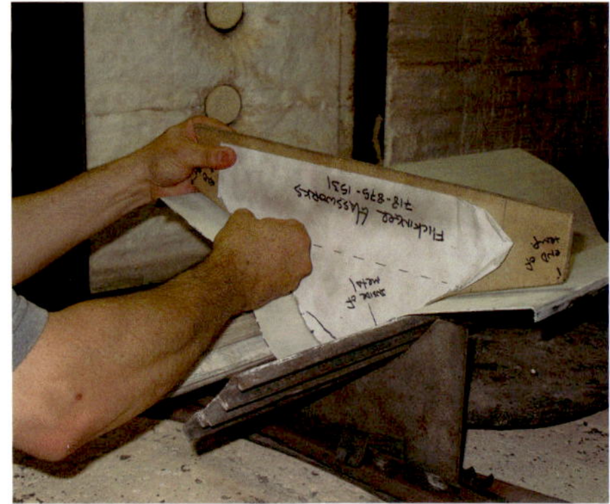

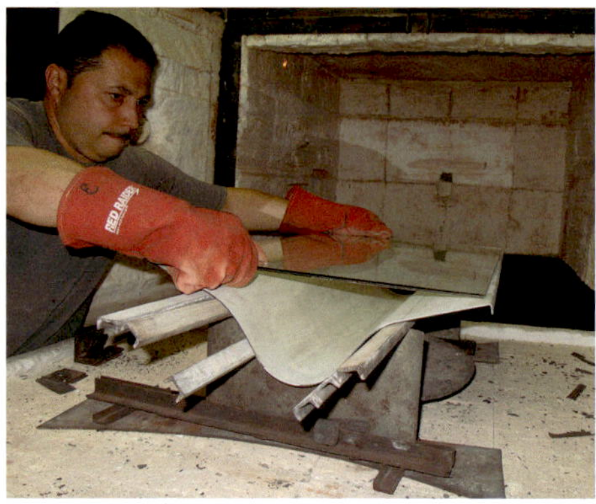

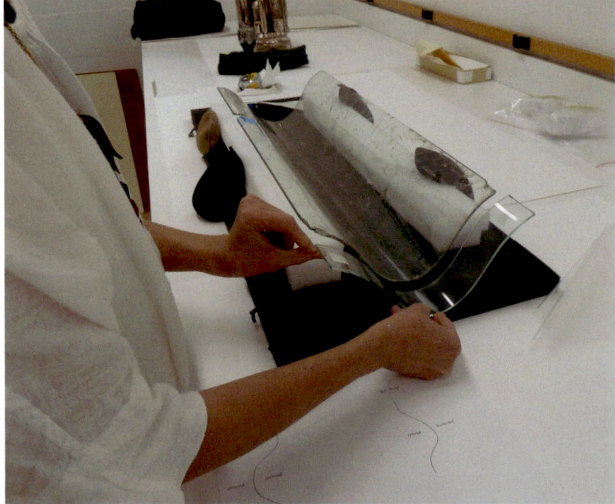

FIGURE 65 A steel mold made from a tracing of the one remaining original glass side panel.

FIGURE 66 A piece of flat glass, which matched the color and thickness of the original panel, placed over the mold and put into a high-temperature kiln, where it would melt and conform to the shape of the mold.

FIGURE 67 One of several sample panels made to determine the accuracy of the mold.

the vitrine arrived at the Museum, one of these panels was missing. To replace it, we turned to a specialty glass company that had the requisite specific expertise.[7] The glassworkers re-created the missing curved glass panel by fabricating one from a profile tracing of the remaining original panel. Using the tracing as a template, a custom steel mold (fig. 65) was made. A piece of flat glass (fig. 66) of a similar color and of the same dimensions as the original was heated in a large kiln until it became flexible and could then be made to conform to the shape of the steel mold (fig. 67), a technique known as *slumping*. Both sides of the vitrine now contain a glass panel: one original to the piece and one that is an accurate replica (fig. 68).

Aside from the missing panel of glass, there were many small broken pieces of glass that were held, much like a stained-glass window, in the metal framework, and these pieces needed stabilizing (figs. 69 and 70). There was also a small loss in the original glass side panel that needed filling. Both types of repair were made with a conservation-grade epoxy that has a similar refractive index to glass, making the repairs and the fill almost invisible.[8]

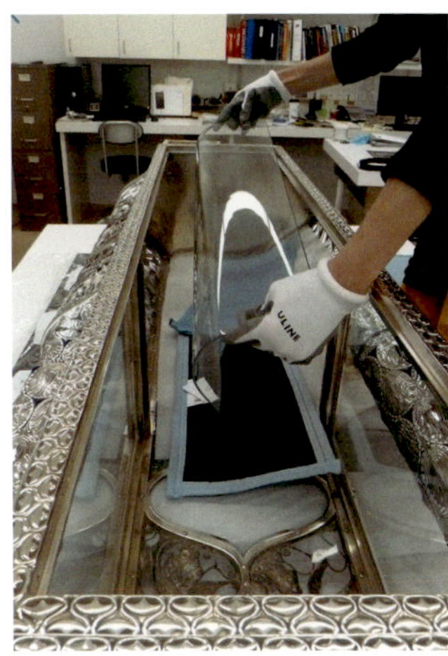

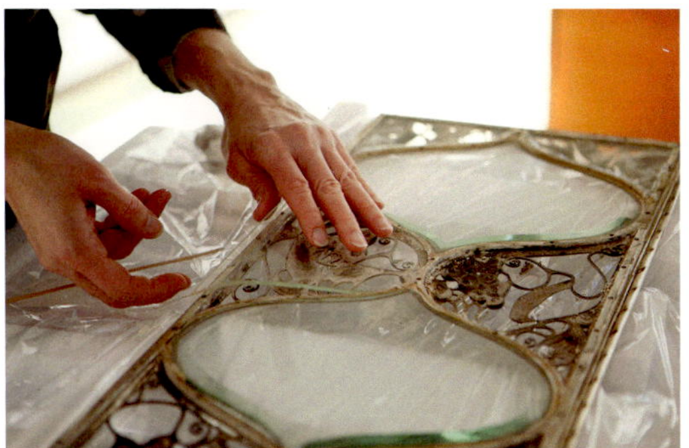

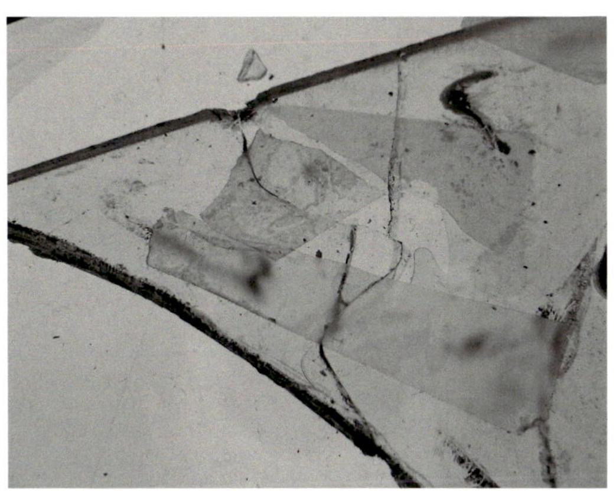

FIGURE 68 The new curved glass panel being checked for fit.

FIGURE 69 Glass panes being removed from a door panel so that they can be cleaned and stabilized.

FIGURE 70 Detail of a pane of glass showing the complex shape of the glass and the numerous cracks in it.

THE WOODEN BASE

The wooden base or socle had been considerably altered in the past. In reviewing a lineage of old photographs and from evidence gathered during the initial examination, we found that it had been altered several times, most likely to suit the tastes of previous owners. The research for this aspect of the restoration was particularly extensive.

When the vitrine arrived at the Museum, it was on a base with a painted veneer, the brush strokes imitating the dramatic patterning of a Macassar ebony wood (fig. 71). Beneath that was a parquetry surface (fig. 72).[9] These veneer surfaces were removed and the original wood substructure revealed.[10] Historic photographs compared with current digital photographs revealed that, along with the alterations, the height of the original base had been reduced (fig. 73). Templates were used to determine the precise shape of the curved profile, and part of the base was reconstructed to restore the missing three inches (fig. 74). Fortunately, at the top edge of the base, there was still a thin strip of original molding, and new Macassar ebony veneer was found that matched its appearance (fig. 75).

A book-matching veneering technique (fig. 76) followed by a traditional hammer veneer method were used to attach the veneer sheets with hot hide glue. A rubber membrane and specially made cauls or

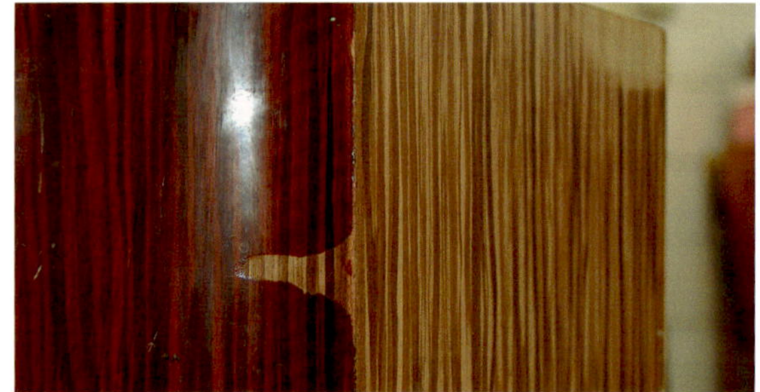

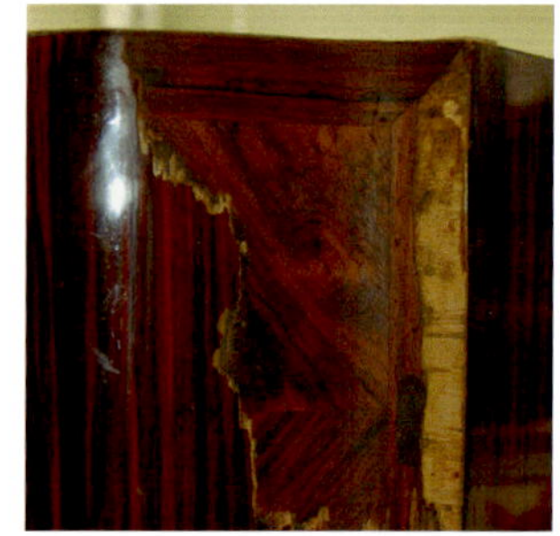

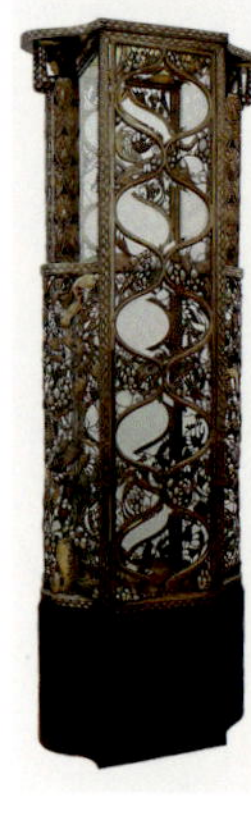

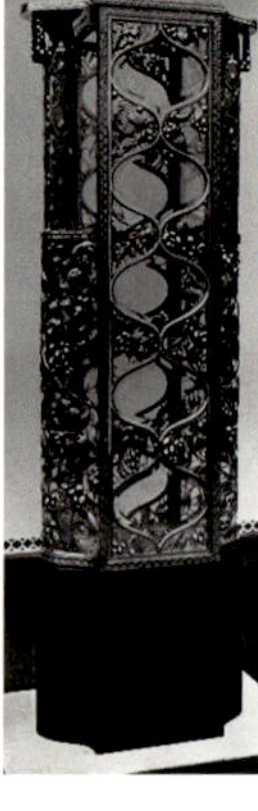

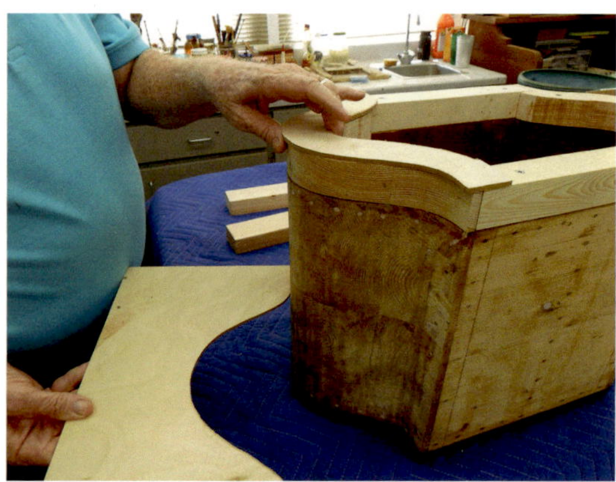

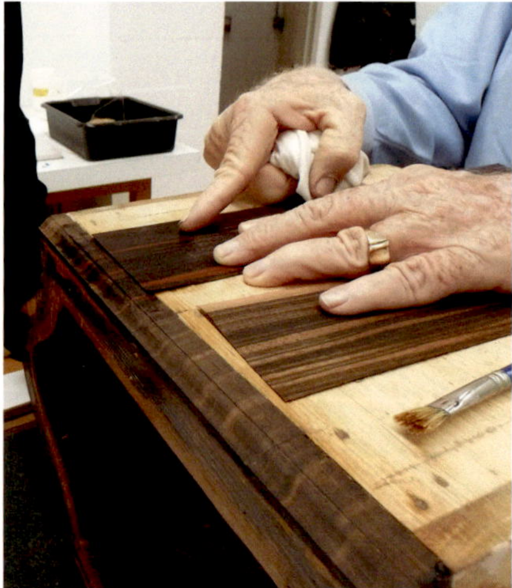

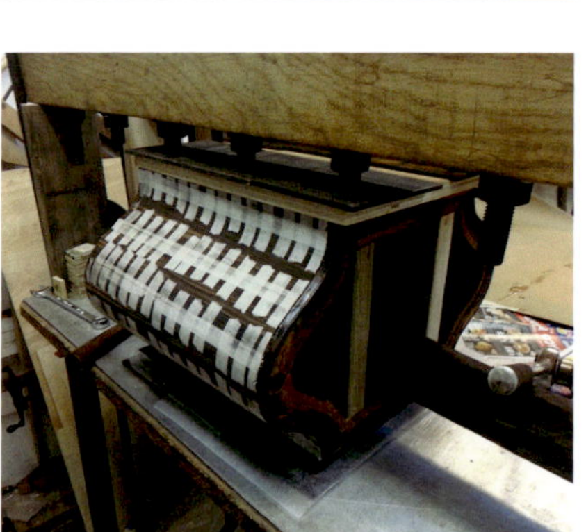

FIGURE 71 Detail of the wooden base of the vitrine showing the faux painted veneer.

FIGURE 72 Detail of the wooden base of the vitrine in 1983, showing the parquetry surface that was covered by the painted veneer.

FIGURE 73 A comparison between a historic photograph (right) and a digital photograph taken at the DMA (left) shows that the vitrine was originally three inches taller.

FIGURE 74 Detail of the base showing the addition to restore the missing three inches that had been sawn off the original substrate.

FIGURE 75 Detail of the base showing the remnant of original Macassar ebony molding, to which the replacement veneer was matched.

FIGURE 76 Detail of the base showing the book-matching veneering technique in progress. Book-matching creates a symmetrical pattern and gives the impression of an opened book.

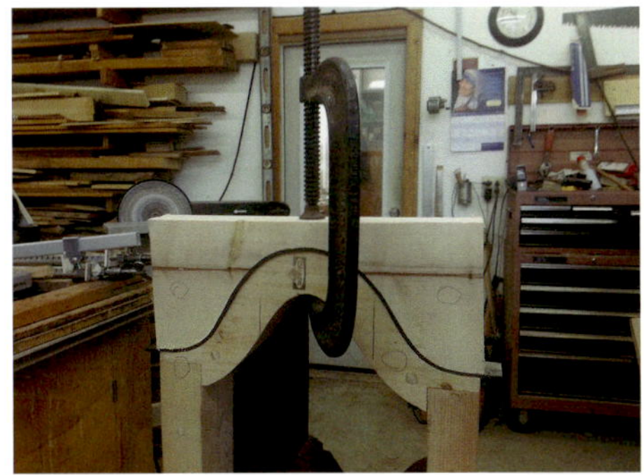

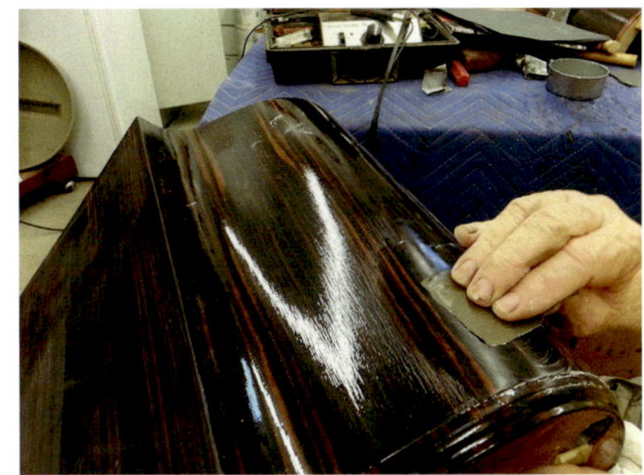

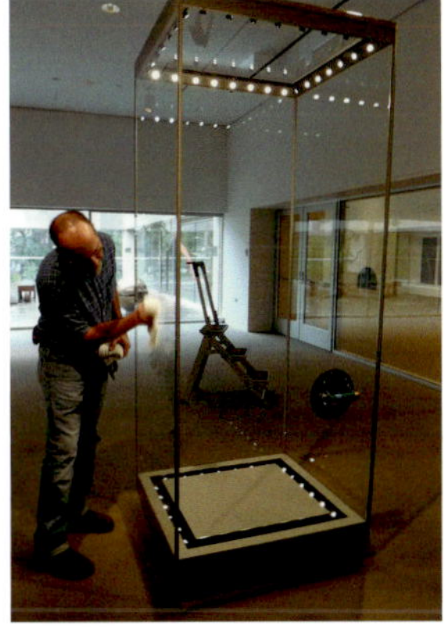

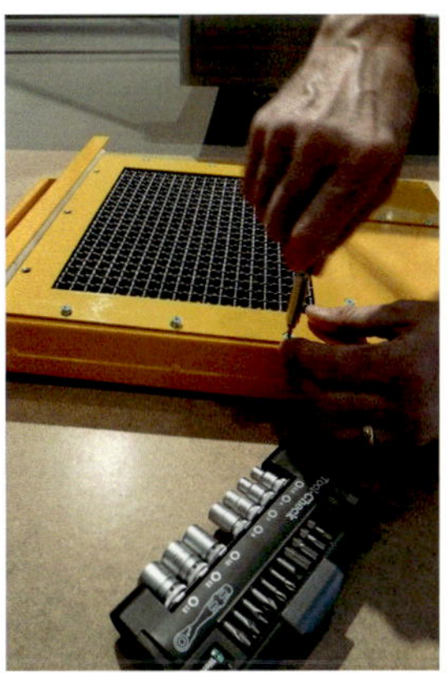

FIGURE 77 Detail of the base being repaired, showing the rubber membrane and specially cut cauls or clamps that were curved to match the profile so as to ensure that the pressure required to attach the new veneer was equalized across the surface of the substrate.

FIGURE 78 Detail of the base showing one of the twelve thin layers of shellac used to finish the new veneer being sanded to a high gloss.

FIGURE 79 The installation of the display case made by Goppion to house the Wittgenstein vitrine.

FIGURE 80 Securing the tray that is placed inside the display case for the vitrine and houses activated carbon cloth to control pollutants.

clamps (curved to match the profile) provided equalized pressure while the veneer was being attached (fig. 77). The base was finished with at least twelve layers of shellac, each layer sanded before the next one was applied—a technique that yields the perfect appearance of the traditional French polish that was once on this piece (fig. 78). The restored base—as it was designed and with an appropriate, beautifully executed Macassar ebony veneering—now conveys the original appearance of the vitrine.

THE EXHIBITION CASE

In some instances, a protective coating can be applied to silver to prevent its tarnishing. This vitrine has, however, not been given a protective coating because of the intricate and complicated nature of the surface and the variety of materials used in its decoration and because it is likely that the coating would fail in places. It is possible, though, to control the environment to minimize tarnishing.

The unique design of our display case for the piece (fig. 79) pairs function and historical precedent, with an aesthetic nod to the original display case that was used when the vitrine was shown, for the first time,

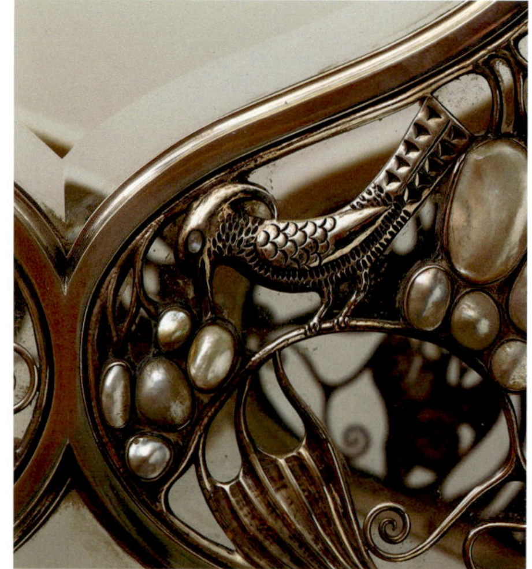
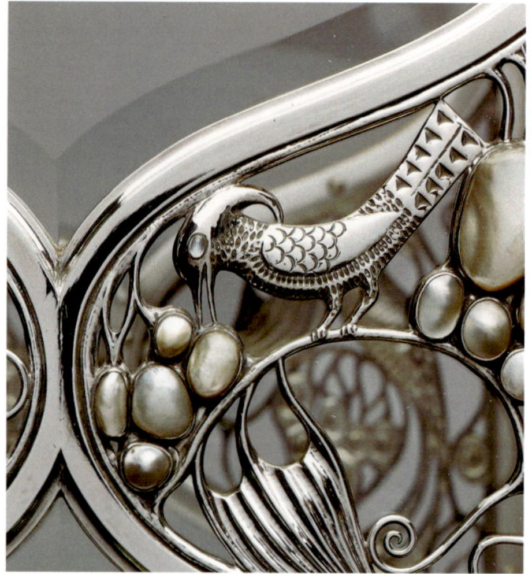
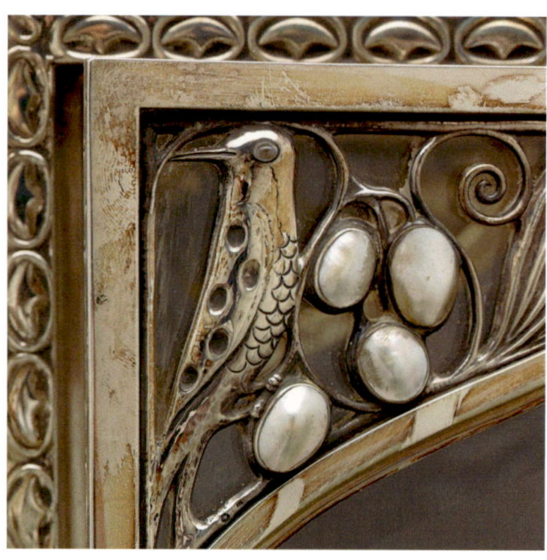
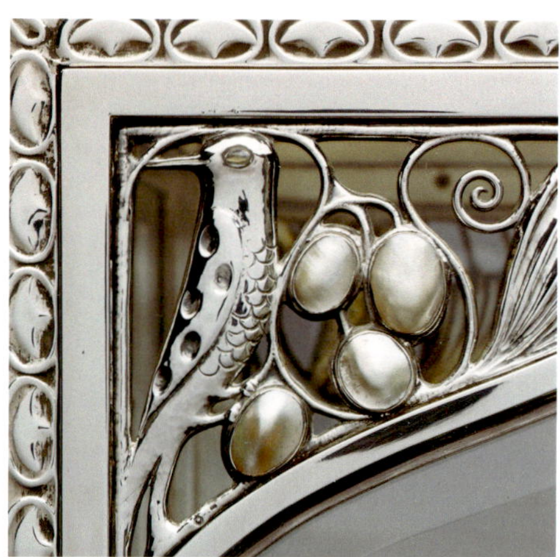

FIGURES 81 AND 82 Details showing a black woodpecker before (left) and after (right) conservation.

FIGURES 83 AND 84 Details showing a magpie before (left) and after (right) conservation.

at the Vienna Kunstschau in 1908. Pollutants are kept out of the compartment where the object is on display. The sealed case includes a filtration system—using activated carbon cloth—in the base (fig. 80). Materials used in the case construction have the lowest levels of emissions of volatile organic compounds (VOCs) currently on the market, and the lights and the fans that circulate the air within the case and through the filter do not produce heat, which is a catalyst for oxidation and degradation.[11]

The conservation treatment concluded in the fall of 2014 with a full series of documentation and publicity photographs of the reassembled vitrine (among them figs. 81–84) taken in the Museum's photography studio. When the new, custom-designed display case arrived from Italy, the vitrine was moved to the Conservation Gallery to be installed as the centerpiece of the exhibition, *Modern Opulence in Vienna: The Wittgenstein*

Vitrine. This ambitious treatment and restoration project was a success because of the effective collaboration among specialists in many fields. The overarching goal of returning this masterpiece, as closely as possible, to its original brilliant appearance in 1908 was met, and the lovely vitrine may now be displayed safely and appreciated for generations into the future.

NOTES

1 An alloy is a mixture of two or more metals (or of a metal and a nonmetal), the resulting compound making use of the individual material properties of each component.

2 Mark Pospisil, the acting curator of minerals at the Perot Museum of Nature and Science in Dallas, Texas, assisted the conservation staff in the identification of the minerals.

3 Chatoyancy is a phenomenon of optical reflectance, known as "cat's eye," and evident as a band of light that appears to move under the surface when the light source moves.

4 A polishing cloth made of cotton velvet; http://www.selvyt.co.uk/.

5 Historically, glazier's putty is a mixture of calcium carbonate (chalk) and a drying oil. Dr. Corina Rogge, the Andrew W. Mellon Research Scientist at the Museum of Fine Arts in Houston, used Fourier transform IR (FT-IR) analysis and confirmed that the putty on the vitrine contained these components.

6 Ubaldo Vitali, the well-known silversmith and conservator, worked with the DMA conservation team to reduce this visually distracting dent.

7 Flickinger Glassworks, Inc., 175 Van Dyke Street, Pier 41, Brooklyn, NY 11232; http://flickingerglassworks.com/.

8 The epoxy, HXTAL NYL-1, is a crystal clear, non-yellowing epoxy adhesive commonly used in conservation because of its optical qualities and longevity; it is available from suppliers of conservation materials.

9 See Sotheby's, New York, *Important Vienna Secessionist Works of Art,* November 19, 1983, lot 500 (auction catalogue), n.p., for the historic photograph showing the false parquetry surface.

10 Alton Bowman, the well-known frame and furniture conservator and maker in Flower Mound, Texas, was contracted to help with the restoration of the wooden base; http://www.altonbowman.com/.

11 Our display case was made by Goppion S.p.A., in Milan, Italy; //www.goppion.com/. The company is well known in the museum field for being sensitive to the special needs of art and artifacts.

PROVENANCE EXHIBITIONS AND LITERATURE

The Wittgenstein Vitrine (for the 1908 Kunstschau, Vienna), 1908

Carl Otto Czeschka, Austrian, 1878–1960, designer
Wiener Werkstätte, Vienna, Austria, 1903–32, maker

WITH

Josef Hoffmann, Austrian, 1870–1956, artistic director; Josef Berger, Austrian, 1874/75–?, goldsmith; Josef Hoszfeld (Hossfeld), Austrian, 1869–1918, Adolf Erbrich, Austrian, 1874–?, Alfred Mayer, Austrian, 1873–?, Alois Wabak, active c. 1905–1929, silversmiths; Josef Weber, dates unknown, cabinetmaker; and Albrech, Plasinsky, and Cerhan (unidentified craftsmen)

Silver, glass, moonstone, opal, lapis lazuli, mother-of-pearl, baroque pearls, onyx, ivory, enamel, and Macassar ebony veneers (replaced) over pine; 66¼ x 24 x 12⅝ in. (168.3 x 61 x 32.1 cm), including base

Dallas Museum of Art, The Eugene and Margaret McDermott Art Fund, Inc.
2013.31.A-E.McD

PROVENANCE

From June 1908: Karl Wittgenstein (1847–1913), Palais Wittgenstein, Vienna, Austria, purchased from the Wiener Werkstätte at the 1908 Kunstschau, for thirty thousand crowns.

Until 1949: his daughter, Mrs. Jerome (Margaret) Stonborough (née Wittgenstein, 1882–1958), New York, New York, by inheritance.

1949–1983: private collection, purchased at auction, Parke-Bernet Galleries, Inc., New York, *French Furniture, Old Vienna, Meissen, Other Porcelain, French and Other Old Faïence, Silver, Decorations: Property of Mrs. Jerome Stonborough, Baron and Baroness Raoul Kuffner de Dioszegh and Other Owners,* March 4, 1949, sale 1045, lot 597, as "Art Nouveau Wrought Silver, Enamel and Mother-of-Pearl Vitrine, by the Wiener Werkstaette."

1983–2013: Benedict Silverman (b. 1929), New York, New York, purchased at auction, Sotheby's, New York, *Important Vienna Secessionist Works of Art,* November 19, 1983, sale 5113, lot 500, as "Fine and Highly Important Jewel-Mounted Silver Vitrine Created for the Kunstschau, Vienna, 1908."

From 2013: Dallas Museum of Art, The Eugene and Margaret McDermott Art Fund, Inc., purchased from Benedict Silverman through Macklowe Gallery (Benjamin Macklowe, president), New York, New York.

EXHIBITIONS

1908: *Kunstschau Wien,* Vienna, June 1–November 16

1986: *Vienna 1900: Art, Architecture, Design,* Museum of Modern Art, New York, July 3–October; cat. illus. p. 97

2002: *Josef Hoffmann: Homes of the Wittgensteins,* Sterling and Francine Clark Art Institute, Williamstown, Massachusetts, June 16–September 2

2003–2005: *Viennese Silver: Modern Design, 1780–1918,* Neue Galerie New York, October 17, 2003–February 15, 2004; Kunsthistorisches Museum, Vienna, November 11, 2004–March 13, 2005; cat. p. 276

2010–11: *Vienna 1900, Klimt, Schiele, and Their Times: A Total Work of Art,* Fondation Beyeler, Riehen, Basel, September 26, 2010–January 16, 2011, cat. p. 221

2014–16: *Modern Opulence in Vienna: The Wittgenstein Vitrine,* Dallas Museum of Art, Dallas, Texas, November 15, 2014–May 29, 2016

LITERATURE, SELECTED

Huey, Michael. *Viennese Silver: Modern Design, 1780–1918.* Exh. cat., Neue Galerie New York, and Kunsthistorisches Museum, Vienna. Ostfildern-Ruit, Germany: Hatje Cantz, 2003; illus. p. 276.

Husslein-Arco, Agnes, and Alfred Weidinger. *Gustav Klimt und die Kunstschau 1908.* Munich: Prestel Verlag, 2008; illus. pp. 448–49.

Natter, Tobias. *Die Welt von Klimt, Schiele und Kokoschka: Sammler und Mäzene.* Cologne: DuMont, 2003, illus. p. 46.

Noever, Peter, et al. *Yearning for Beauty: The Wiener Werkstätte and the Stoclet House.* Exh. cat., Centre for Fine Arts, Brussels, in association with MAK, Vienna. Ostfildern-Ruit, Germany: Hatje Cantz, 2006, illus. p. 81.

Schweiger, Werner. *Wiener Werkstaette: Design in Vienna, 1903–1932.* Translated by Alexander Lieven. New York: Abbeville Press, 1984, illus. p. 81, bottom.

Steffen, Brenda. *Vienna 1900, Klimt, Schiele, and Their Times: A Total Work of Art.* Exh. cat. Riehen, Basel, Switzerland: Beyeler Museum, 2010, illus. p. 221.

Utitz, Emil. "Der Neue Stil. Asthetische Glossen." *Deutsche Kunst und Dekoration* 23 (1908–1909), illus. p. 74.

———. "Münchens Ernte 1908." *Deutsche Kunst und Dekoration* 23 (1908–1909), illus. pp. 168, 170, 171, and 173.

Varnedoe, Kirk. *Vienna 1900: Art, Architecture, Design.* Exh. cat. New York: Museum of Modern Art, 1986, illus. p. 97.

REFERENCES

ARCHIVE

Archiv der Wiener Werkstätte, Austrian Museum of Applied Arts (MAK), Vienna.

Nachlass Carl Otto Czeschka, Archiv, Museum für Kunst und Gewerbe, Hamburg, Germany.

BOOKS AND PERIODICALS

Adlmann, Jan Ernst. *Vienna Moderne, 1898–1918: An Early Encounter between Taste and Utility.* Exh. cat., Sarah Campbell Blaffer Gallery, University of Houston. Houston, Tex.: The Gallery, 1978.

"Ausstellung." *Die Werkkunst* 3 (October 1907–September 1908), p. 319.

Bailey, Colin B., and John Bruce Collins. *Gustav Klimt: Modernism in the Making.* Exh. cat., National Gallery of Canada, Ottawa. New York: Abrams, 2001.

Baum, Julius. "Wiener Werkstätte Neustiftgasse 32." *Deutsche Kunst und Dekoration* 19 (1906–1907), pp. 443–56.

Breicha, Otto, ed. *Altkunst-Neukunst: Wien, 1894–1908.* 1909. Reprint, Klagenfurt, Austria: Ritter Verlag, 1986.

Crawford, Alan. *C. R. Ashbee: Architect, Designer and Romantic Socialist.* New Haven: Yale University Press, 1985.

Fanelli, Giovanni. *Carl Otto Czeschka dalla Secessione Viennese all'Art Déco.* Florence: Cantini, 1990.

Hevesi, Ludwig. "C. O. Czeschka" (August 9, 1907), pp. 236–40, and "Kunstschau 1908" (May 31, 1908), pp. 315–16. In *Altkunst-Neukunst: Wien, 1894–1908,* edited by Otto Breicha. 1909. Reprint, Klagenfurt, Austria: Ritter Verlag, 1986.

———. "Kunstschau 1908." *Kunst und Kunsthandwerk: Monatsschrift des k.k. Österreichisches Museum für Kunst und Industrie* 11 (1908), p. 396.

———. "Kunstschau Wien 1908." *Zeitschrift für bildende Kunst* 19, no. 43 (1908), pp. 245–54.

Hohe Warte 1. Leipzig and Vienna: R. Voigtländers Verlag, 1904–1905.

Huey, Michael, ed. *Viennese Silver: Modern Design, 1780–1918.* Exh. cat., Neue Galerie New York, and Kunsthistorisches Museum, Vienna. Ostfildern-Ruit, Germany: Hatje Cantz, 2003.

"Kassette für den Kaiser von Oesterreich." *Deutsche Kunst und Dekoration* 19 (1906–1907), pp. 416–20.

Levetus, A. S. "The 'Wiener Werkstätte,' Vienna." *The Studio: An Illustrated Magazine of Fine and Applied Art* 52, no. 217 (April 15, 1911), pp. 187–96.

Loos, Adolph. *Ornament and Crime: Selected Essays.* Edited by Adolf Opel. Riverside, Calif.: Ariadne Press, 1998.

Schmuttermeier, Elisabeth. "Die Wiener Werkstätte auf der Kunstschau 1908," pp. 434–41. In *Gustav Klimt und die Kunstschau 1908,* edited by Agnes Husslein-Arco and Alfred Weidinger. Exh. cat., Belvedere, Vienna. Munich: Prestel Verlag 2008.

Schweiger, Werner J. *Wiener Werkstaette: Design in Vienna, 1903–1932.* Translated by Alexander Lieven. New York: Abbeville Press, 1984.

Siller, Senta. "Carl Otto Czeschka, 1878–1960: Leben und Werk." PhD diss. Technical University of Berlin, 1992.

Sotheby's, New York. *Important Vienna Secessionist Works of Art.* November 19, 1983, lot 500. Auction catalogue.

Spielmann, Heinz. *Jahrbuch der Hamburger Kunstsammlungen.* Vol. 20. Hamburg: Dr. Ernst Hauswedell & Co. Verlag, 1975.

———. *Carl Otto Czeschka: Aspekte seines Lebenswerkes.* Hamburg: Interversa, 1978.

———. *Die Jugendstil—Sammlung 1: Künstler A–F.* Hamburg: Museum für Kunst und Gewerbe, 1979.

———, and Hella Häussler. *Carl Otto Czeschka, 1878–1960: Ein Wiener Künstler und die Hamburger Wirtschaft.* Hamburg: Handelskammer with the Elsbeth Weichmann Gesellschaft, 2011.

Utitz, Emil. "Münchens Ernte 1908." *Deutsche Kunst und Dekoration* 23 (1908–1909), pp. 164–74.

Varnedoe, Kirk. *Vienna 1900: Art, Architecture, and Design.* Exh. cat. New York: Museum of Modern Art, 1986.

"Welche Mittel hat der für das Kunstgewerbe entwerfende Künstler, . . ." *Deutsche Kunst und Dekoration* 19 (1906–1907), illus. p. 466.

Witt-Dörring, Christian. "Individuality in Viennese Modern Design around 1900: Pro and Con, " pp. 58–119. In *Birth of the Modern: Style and Identity in Vienna, 1900,* edited by Jill Lloyd and Christian Witt-Dörring. Exh. cat., Neue Galerie New York. Munich: Hirmer Verlag, 2011.

———, et al. *Koloman Moser: Designing Modern Vienna, 1897–1907.* Exh. cat., Neue Galerie New York. New York: Prestel Verlag, 2013.

Zuckerkandl, Berta. "Die Ausstellung der Klimt-Gruppe." *Wiener Allgemeine Zeitung,* November 2, 1907, p. 7.

PHOTOGRAPHY CREDITS

All photography, unless otherwise noted below or in captions accompanying the images, is © 2015 Dallas Museum of Art.

Endsheets: © MAK/Katrin Wisskirchen
Fig. 1: © MAK
Fig. 2: © MAK
Fig. 3: ÖNB Vienna, LSCH 186C
Fig. 4: © MAK
Fig. 5: © Yves Macaux—Paso Doble
Fig. 6: © Yves Macaux—Paso Doble
Fig. 7: © Asenbaum Photo Archive
Fig. 8: © MAK
Fig. 9: © Wien Museum
Fig. 10: © MAK
Fig. 11: © MAK/Georg Mayer
Fig. 12: © The Art Institute of Chicago
Fig. 13: © The Art Institute of Chicago
Fig. 14: © MAK/Georg Mayer
Fig. 15: © IMAGNO/Austrian Archives
Fig. 16: Courtesy of the Theaterwissenschaftliche Sammlung, University of Cologne
Fig. 18: Courtesy of the Museum für Kunst und Gewerbe, Hamburg
Fig. 19: Courtesy of the Aichi Prefectural Museum of Art, Japan
Fig. 20: © MAK/Georg Mayer
Fig. 21. ÖNB Vienna, Pf 31931:B2a
Fig. 22: © Yves Macaux—Paso Doble
Fig. 23: © MAK
Fig. 24: Courtesy of the Galerie bei der Albertina, Vienna
Fig. 25: © MAK
Fig. 28: © MAK
Fig. 29: © Wien Museum
Fig. 31: © MAK
Fig. 32: © MAK
Fig. 34: © MAK
Fig. 35: © MAK
Fig. 36: © MAK
Fig. 37: © MAK
Fig. 39: Bridgeman Images
Fig. 40: © MAK
Fig. 41: Courtesy of the Museum für Kunst und Gewerbe, Hamburg
Fig. 42: © MAK/Georg Mayer
Fig. 43: ÖNB Vienna, 294383D
Fig. 51: Reprinted from Waltraud Neuwirth, *Wiener Jugendstilsilber: Original, Fälschung oder Pasticcio?* (Vienna: W. Neuwirth, 1980), p. 87; courtesy of Dr. Waltraud Neuwirth
Fig. 73 (right): Reproduced from *Deutsche Kunst und Dekoration* 23, 1908–1909, p. 168

We greatly respect the protected status of all copyrighted material. We have endeavored, with due diligence, to identify and contact each copyright owner. In some cases we have been unable to trace current copyright holders. We welcome notification and will correct errors in subsequent editions.

The exhibition *Modern Opulence in Vienna: The Wittgenstein Vitrine*, from November 15, 2014, to May 29, 2016, was organized by the Dallas Museum of Art.

Conservation and technical study of the Wittgenstein Vitrine was supported by a generous grant from the Bank of America Art Conservation Project.

Bank of America

Published by the Dallas Museum of Art
www.DMA.org

Distributed by Yale University Press, New Haven and London
www.yalebooks.com/art

Produced by Marquand Books, Inc., Seattle
www.marquand.com

Edited by Frances Bowles
Proofread by Barbara I. Bowen
Dr. Schmuttermeier's introduction translated from the German by Russell Stockman; additional translation from the German by Fiona Bowles
Designed by Ryan Polich
Typeset in Ideal Sans and Anisette by Maggie Lee
Image management by iocolor, Seattle
Printed and bound in China by Artron Art Group

Front and back covers, and pages 2–3, 10, 14, and 40–66 (details): Carl Otto Czeschka, The Wittgenstein Vitrine, 1908. Silver, glass, moonstone, opal, lapis lazuli, mother-of-pearl, baroque pearls, onyx, ivory, enamel and Macassar ebony veneers (replaced) over pine. Dallas Museum of Art, The Eugene and Margaret McDermott Art Fund, Inc. 2013.31.A-EMcD

Endsheets: Carl Otto Czeschka, *Bavaria* wallpaper pattern, 1913. Paper and wood. MAK: Austrian Museum of Applied Arts/Contemporary Art, Vienna (WI 1563); adaptation courtesy of MAK

Library of Congress
Cataloging-in-Publication Data
Dallas Museum of Art.
The Wittgenstein vitrine: modern opulence in Vienna/Kevin W. Tucker; with contributions by Fran Baas and Elisabeth Schmuttermeier.
pages cm
Includes bibliographical references.
ISBN 978-0-300-21457-4 (hardback)
1. Czeschka, Carl Otto, 1878–1960. Wittgenstein vitrine—Exhibitions. 2. Silverwork—Austria—Vienna—History—20th century—Exhibitions. 3. Wiener Werkstätte—Exhibitions. 4. Art objects—Conservation and restoration—Texas—Dallas—Exhibitions. 5. Art objects—Texas—Dallas—Exhibitions. 6. Display cases—Texas—Dallas—Exhibitions. I. Tucker, Kevin W., author. II. Schmuttermeier, Elisabeth, writer of introduction. III. Baas, Fran. Look inside. IV. Title.
NK7198.C95A78 2016
739.2'384—dc23

2015026072

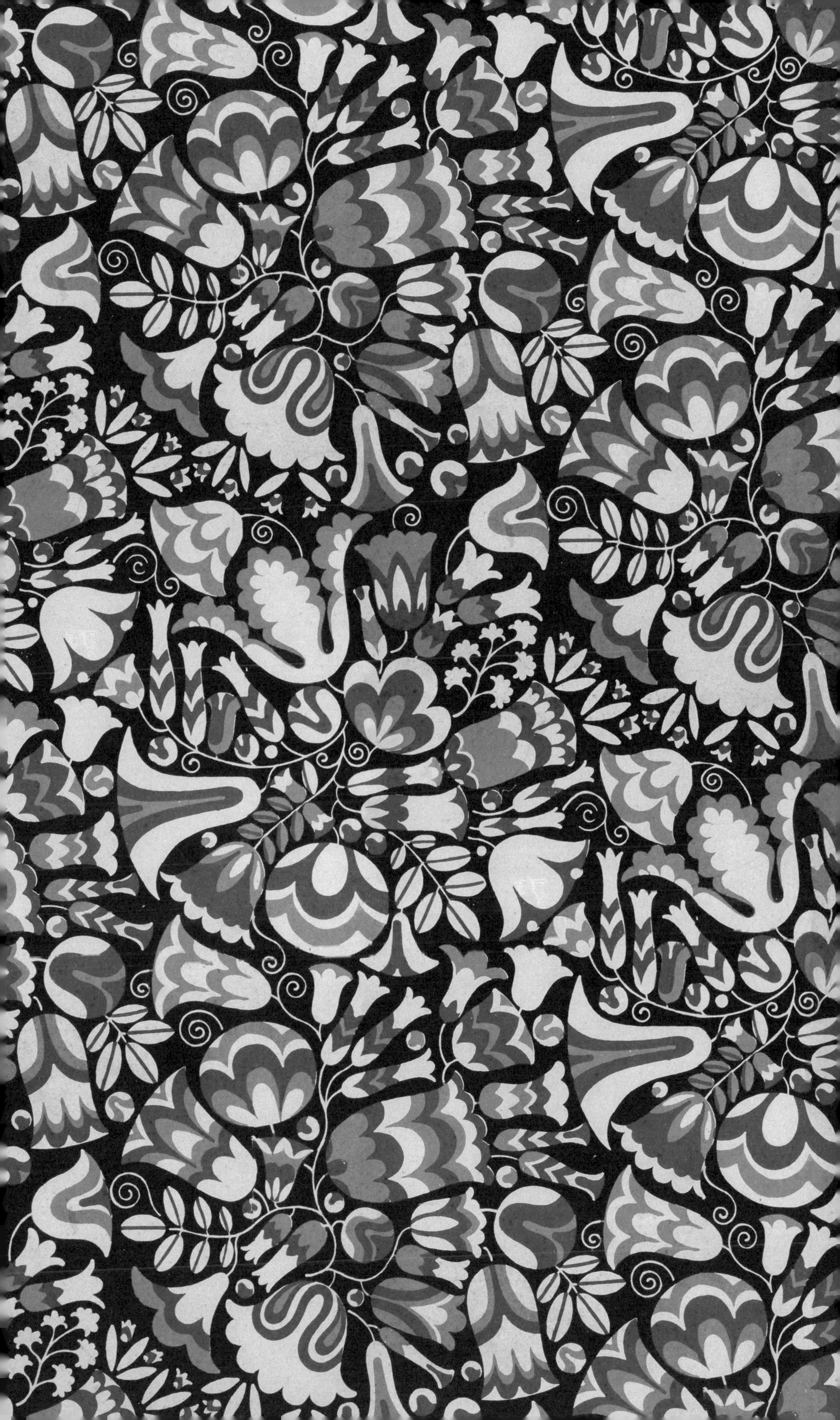

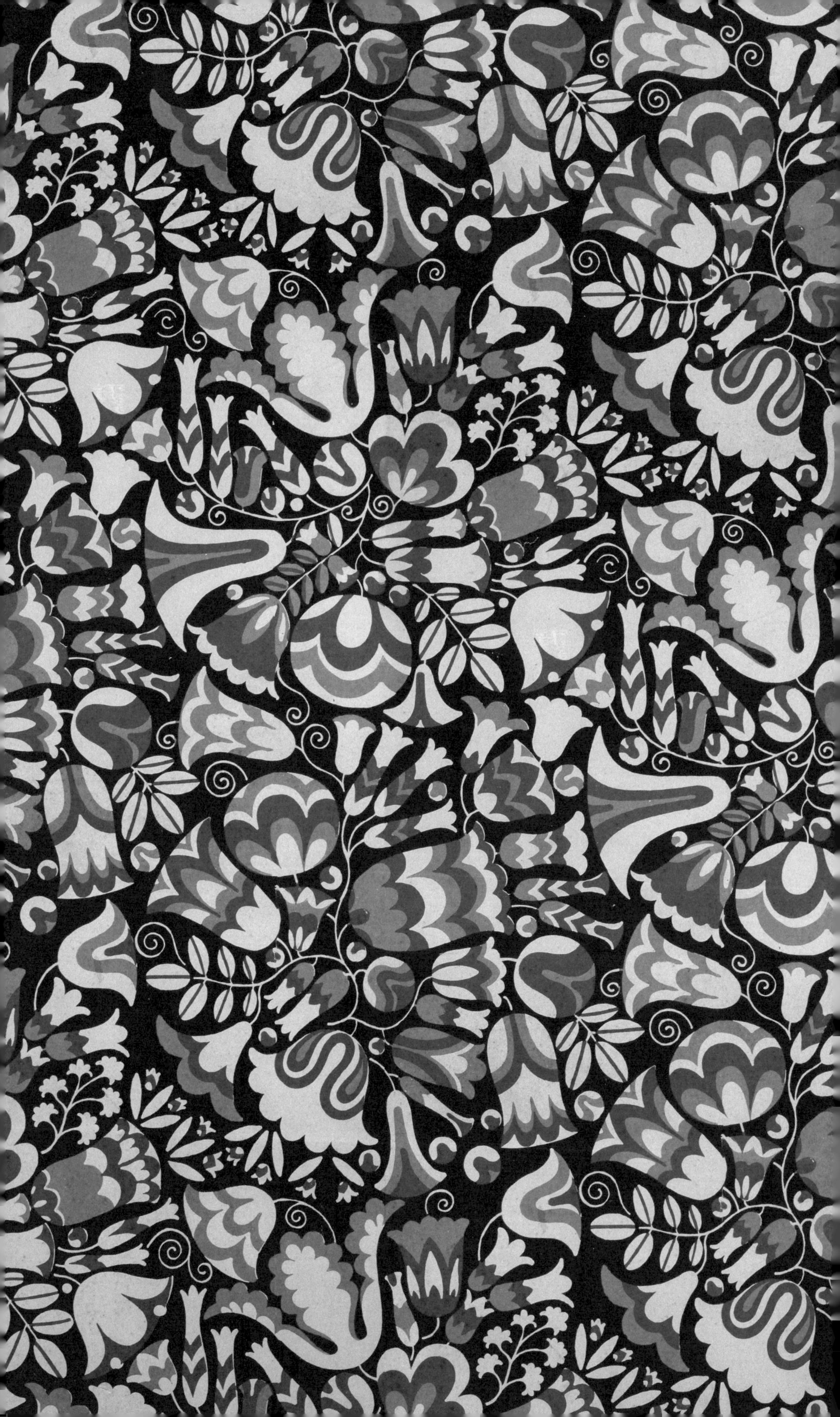